FADE

FADE

*How to experience joy and find hope
no matter the circumstances*

BY JAMES SRODULSKI

XULON PRESS

Xulon Press
2301 Lucien Way #415
Maitland, FL 32751
407.339.4217
www.xulonpress.com

Paperback ISBN-13: 978-1-6628-4325-9
Ebook ISBN-13: 978-1-6628-4326-6

My pastor always told me, 'Be kind to everyone because everyone is having a hard time.' He was correct. James Srodulski, my friend and fellow pastor, provides help for us all in his book, FADE: How To Experience Joy and Find Hope No Matter the Circumstances. With the mind of a workman that accurately handles the Word and the compassion of a pastor, James unfolds the riches of the book of 1 Peter to resource us as we face the daily grind. Read this book!"

- Keith Moore, Senior Pastor,
Dogwood Church

Most of us at some point in life experience a situation where we feel like we are in great danger, or we are terrified or just have zero control over our circumstances. In short, we just seem to have no options and this condition produces great stress in our lives. We can't run and hide, and we can't stand and fight. Worry and fear overtake us and we lose our ability to cope. In "FADE: How to Expereince Joy and Find Hope No Matter the Circumstances", my friend James Srodulski offers just that - HOPE. With a pastor's heart and a surgeon's skill, Srodulski shows how we need to shift our focus from things that can be lost to things that can never be lost. I highly recommend this extremely well written and engaging work. It will feed your soul and encourage your heart.

Dr. David S. Parks Executive Pastor,
Shandon Baptist Church - Columbia SC

We all experience trials of some sort. We are only lying to ourselves if we say that we haven't or aren't dealing with something. In FADE – How to experience joy and find hope no matter the circumstances, James Srodulski tackles how to find joy regardless of what you are going through in your life. James does a masterful job of weaving in personal stories that are relevant to today while staying true to the Word of God. Anybody who reads this book will get much out of each chapter and find it a joy to read and not a chore. Experience Joy and Find Hope in your life - start by reading FADE!

Dr. Michael Moore, Senior Pastor/Church Planter,
Beacon Hill Church, Hopewell, VA

ACKNOWLEDGEMENTS

First, I would like to thank my wife, best friend, and partner in the ministry. Yes, they're all the same person! Cara has been, and continues to be, an integral part of everything God has done in and through me. Her support and encouragement have enabled me to continue forward when disappointment and discouragement have weighed me down.

Second, I have had several men who have mentored and poured into me that have shaped me into the man I am today. Consequently, their influence on my life is felt all throughout these pages. Pastor Tommy Watson taught me the value of hard work, loyalty, and believing in a BIG GOD. He allowed me to accompany him on many adventures around the world, and his faith taught me that God is bigger than any circumstance. Dr. Jim Plinton, the first African-American senior executive and vice president of a major airline (first Continental and then Eastern) taught me the value of justice, compassion, and forgiveness. He was a brilliant man who loved the Lord and showed me that ministry belonged in the hands of everyday people.

And then there is Dr. Rick Blackwood, who helped refine in me a love of Scripture. He taught me that the Bible is sufficient and showed me that all of life can and should be filtered through the truth of Scripture. This is because it is God's Word and can be trusted. His ability to "rightly divide" God's Word and make it relatable changed the trajectory of my ministry and played a major impact in the writing of this book, including the underlying premise that we need to focus our lives on the things we cannot lose in this life nor the next.

Finally, I would like to acknowledge all of my Luther Rice Seminary professors, commentary writers, pastors, and preachers I have had the privilege of studying under, listening to, and learning from. Everything learned here has been because of the hard work and faithful interpretation of Scripture by countless persons determined to rightly divide the Word of God. We all stand upon their shoulders and benefit from their collective wisdom, knowledge, and ability to communicate the eternal truths of Scripture.

TABLE OF CONTENTS

INTRODUCTION

———◆———

Friday, January 13, 2017: the Obama-Trump transition teams run a pandemic-preparedness exercise.[1]

October 2019: The Trump administration concludes a months-long simulation designed to respond to a global influenza pandemic. The Department of Health and Human Services determines that the United States is under-prepared, under-funded, and under-coordinated to fight an influenza-like pandemic. [2]

November 17, 2019: Possibly the first case of COVID-19 emerges in Hubei Province, China. [3]

December 31, 2019: Wuhan officials confirm treatment of dozens of individuals with pneumonia from an unknown cause...[4]

April 15, 2020: 614,117 coronavirus cases in the U.S. 26,059 dead and over 16,000,000 unemployed in the United States. [5]

What do you do when you can't run and you can't fight? For the average American, this pandemic presented an impossible-to-navigate scenario. We were all used to decisions being made in Washington that inevitably would impact us, but this pandemic was different, coming on too quickly for almost any of us to adjust to. Before we knew it, we were all being told where and when we could go out. We were being expected to "social distance" (that should be the phrase of the year), whatever that means!

Fear took over the national psyche, and soon toilet paper and hand sanitizer were harder to come by than almost any precious metal. The news of the virus dominated television and computer screens 24/7, and it almost felt like Vietnam all over again with the daily briefings telling us how many Americans had died and the numbers of sick in the hospitals.

The problem was for the vast majority of us, this was an enemy we were totally unprepared to fight. Traditional weapons were of no use! We couldn't send troops to fight it. Money couldn't solve it either. There was no buying our way out of this predicament. This virus was an equal opportunity destroyer, affecting celebrities and soccer moms alike. There was no discrimination in COVID-19: rich, poor, black, white, Asian, Middle Eastern. You name it, every socio-economic class and demographic was affected. And not only could we not fight it, there was nowhere to run either.

According to the Wall Street Journal article: Science Closes In on Covid's Origins - Four studies—including two from the WHO—provide powerful evidence favoring the lab-leak theory, by Richard Muller and Steven Quay, evidence strongly suggests that this pandemic most likely began in a virology lab in Wuhan, China.[6] From there it quickly spread to every part of the globe. Eventually no place on earth was safe from it.

So what is the child of God to do when you can't fight back and you can't run? Is there any hope in the midst of seemingly impossible circumstances such as this? Do not fear! God has poured His Word out and, consequently, into our lives for times such as these.

"In FADE – How to experience joy and find hope, no matter the circumstances," my hope is to help you apply these same truths from God's Word to your lives today. While this isn't a self-help book intended to encourage you to pull yourself up by your own bootstraps, it is an exhortation to keep at the things God wants us to focus our energy and lives on. By intentionally concentrating on and applying these four traits: Focus, Attitude, Discipline and Endurance, to your life, I am convinced that God wants you to experience joy and find hope – no matter the circumstances! In fact, in John 10:7-10 we're promised just that as Jesus tells us that He came to give us access to an abundant life.[7]

Now no one is ever going to mistake me for a physician. In fact, back when I was a sophomore in high school, I selected an anatomy course to fulfill my science requirement for that year. However, the powers that be decided that anyone interested enough to take anatomy should take physics first. So, being the rebellious teenager that I was, I opted to take a different course and missed out on anatomy altogether! Really, I was just fascinated by the intricacies of human physiology and wanted to know more about how our systems worked but unfortunately, I didn't want to know enough to have to endure physics first... fast forward a number of years (no one's telling how many!), and I find that my fascination with the human systems hasn't abated. I've "discovered" a few things along the way – things like the fact that sitting on top of our kidneys are these really small (about 2" in diameter) organs called the adrenal glands.

These glands exude a fluid hormone known as, wait for it... adrenaline. Adrenaline is the body's way of helping you to adjust to sudden situations of stress. For example, when you become very angry or when you are really frightened, the adrenal glands infuse larger-than-normal amounts of adrenaline into your bloodstream. This then causes your body to react in several ways:

1. It increases the velocity of your heart rate.
2. It raises your blood pressure.
3. It rapidly speeds up the conversion of glycogen into glucose, which produces energy that flows to your muscles and allows you to physically react to the stressors at hand and energizes you for sudden strenuous activity.[8]

When this adrenaline is released into your bloodstream, it prepares you to do one of two things: stand and fight or run and flee. You may know it as the fight-or-flight syndrome. Your heart rate speeds up and your blood pressure rises. And the sugary energy source known as glucose is released into your muscles, enabling you to stand or run.

But what do you suppose would happen if you faced a situation that brought great stress on you because you perceived there was danger or you experienced great fear and you realized you had NO CONTROL over the situation? In other words, you couldn't stand and fight, and neither could you run and flee. You're afraid and sudden, intense worry overtakes you. As a result, you are stressed beyond your ability to cope and are probably even angry. The adrenaline kicks in and your heart rate jumps suddenly. You can feel your blood pressure rising in the veins of your neck... you want to fight, or you want to run, but because of the circumstances you can't do either.

What I've just done is describe a predicament. It's a scenario where you perceive that you have no good options and no chance of maneuvering through successfully. This inability to produce a meaningful response, along with that sudden flow of adrenaline, can lead to stress and even damage to your heart.

Here's what else is true: Predicaments with no apparent options can also lead to a miserable state of insecurity as well. Prolonged bouts of insecurity can, in turn, lead to feelings of hopelessness and despair.[9] The question then becomes, "How do we cope with a situation that we can't change or avoid?" I mean, just how is someone supposed to deal with the situation?

The great news is that this is exactly the point of this little letter written almost two thousand years ago from the apostle Peter to a group of believers who were experiencing just such a predicament. They were afraid; they were angry; they were incredibly stressed and, at the same time, completely powerless to affect their situation. They had no options and consequently were in very real danger of moving into deep despair and losing all hope. Because of this little letter to these early Christians, we get to peek over their shoulders as they received it and see how God counteracted their despair with divinely ordained words of hope!

Now before we jump into the "how," I want to share a principle that, though not expressly stated, is found all throughout this letter. And it's just this: Insecurity, despair, and hopelessness occurs when we place our hope in things we can lose... jobs, people, money, careers, friendships, freedom, health, life, marriage, family, etc. But peace, security, hope and joy come when we place our trust in things we cannot lose. Things like the Word of God, Jesus, salvation, eternal life, and heaven.

Peter's letter redirects his readers' focus away from their current situations and circumstances and toward things they can never lose. By doing so, he encourages them to embrace the hope, peace and joy that is available to all who are children of God.

CHAPTER 1

THE SITUATION AT HAND

W e get an idea of just how dire the situation was for these early Christians by taking a look at the first verse. "Peter, an apostle of Jesus Christ, To God's elect, exiles scattered throughout the provinces of Pontus, Galatia, Cappadocia, Asia and Bithynia" (1 Pet. 1:1, NIV).

The key word for us in that verse is "scattered." It's translated from the compound Greek word "diaspora" (diaspora). "Dia" means through or throughout and "spora" carries the idea of scattering a seed over a field. So diaspora literally means to scatter seeds throughout a field from one end to another. In the technical sense, this word was brought over to describe the scattering of the Jewish race across the known world.[10]

Just a cursory look at history reveals that the Jewish race has been under intense persecution like no other race in history. It seems one holocaust was soon followed by another one... the Egyptians, Assyrians, Babylonians, Medes & Persians, Greeks, Romans, and then the

Germans have all sought to annihilate this chosen race of God's people. As the Jewish state of Israel was conquered, the victorious nations would then force the Jewish people from their lands. Sometimes this took the form of captivity and slavery, while other times they were scattered to avoid further persecution and shame.

Possibly one of the most intense scatterings came about as a result of the Roman army's crushing of a Jewish uprising in AD 70. Josephus, a Jewish historian, estimates that over 1,100,000 Jews were killed during this rebellion. The remaining population was driven out of Israel and into and among the nations of Europe, Asia, and Asia Minor.[11]

The Jews became like gypsies. I don't know if you've ever seen gypsies in their environment. I had an opportunity to experience them firsthand in 1989 when I travelled to Romania, following the fall of the dictatorship of Nicolae Ceausescu. Our team was in the country bringing relief supplies to the pastors and people in the Christian churches. While there, we had to make our way through Transylvania; it was there we first encountered gypsies. It was as if we had entered a time warp of sorts. They were travelling in their covered wagons and dressed just like you've seen depicted on TV. And yes, others scorned them all throughout the country.

That was the social status of the Jews following the rebellion of AD 70. They were looked down upon, and wherever they set up camp and tried to call home, they were hated and despised. But the insult doesn't end there for the recipients of this precious letter. Not only were these people Jewish, but they were Christians as well! People from all these provinces mentioned in this first verse: Pontus, Galatia, Cappadocia, Asia, and Bithynia, would potentially have been present in Jerusalem during that first Pentecost. They may have heard the apostle Peter preach and, doubtless, some of these people would have been converted to Christianity. Consequently, they would have taken their newfound faith back to these same provinces. Additionally, the apostle Paul had travelled this region extensively, planting churches along the way, and many Gentiles had been converted.

It is to this disparate group of believers that Peter addresses his letter. These were people who had recognized and accepted Jesus as the promised Messiah and taken Him as Lord and Savior. It was precisely this commitment to Christ that made their lives even more problematic!

July 19, AD 64 is recorded in history as the day Rome burned. The city was divided into fourteen districts and by the time the fire was subdued, it had consumed three of those districts entirely. Not unlike many European cities, Rome was a city of narrow streets. And on both sides of these streets were high, wooden houses where it is estimated over 1,000,000 people lived. Once the fire began, it was able to leap across the streets and quickly spread, consuming everything in its path, including people, like kindling. It is recorded that once a fire was extinguished, another one would pop up nearby. Historians tell us that Nero had a front row seat in the Tower of Massinus and was reportedly "charmed by the flames."[12]

Many Roman citizens and visitors to the city perished that night. Religious shrines were consumed as well. The temples of Luna, Aira Maxima, Jupiter, and the Shrine of Vestra all went up in flames and were ultimately destroyed. People lost their homes, possessions, and even loved ones to the conflagration. Assuredly many, if not most, were rocked to their core! The flames had consumed their gods, resulting in a loss of faith and stability. Consequently, their resentment ran deep toward whomever was at fault. Being a shrewd politician, Nero sensed this resentment and quickly acted to redirect the building hostility.

Unfortunately, for the believers of the time, he found his scapegoat in the Christians living in Rome. There were already well-established perceptions and opinions of this off-shoot of the Jewish religion. Jews didn't worship like other Roman citizens did. They didn't abide by the normal polytheism of the day, making them seem strange to ordinary citizens.

Additionally, many myths had sprung up regarding the Christian faith. For example, they were believed to be cannibals because of misconceptions regarding the Lord's supper and the description of "eating the body and drinking the blood of Jesus." One perception that was true, was that Christians were accused of dividing homes and families. Many wives had come to faith separate from their unbelieving husbands, this is seen as an affront to the men of the day. Women were not to act independently from their husbands, which caused all types of issues between married couples.

To be certain, this persecution started slowly and took some time to spread across the empire. However, by the time AD 70 came around and the Jewish population was scattered across the known world, it was in high gear! Places like those mentioned in our first verse (Pontus, Galatia, Cappadocia, Asia, and Bithynia) were not spared.

The persecution of Christians took many forms. Nero is said to have nailed Christians to crosses, racked and boiled them alive. Some were subjected to being covered in pitch and set ablaze to light the gardens for his parties. Others were sewn up into animal skins and thrown to wild dogs.[13],[14]

Understandably, once this suffering began to make inroads into these provinces, debilitating fear began to settle on the Christians living there. Adrenaline began to flow as the anxiety built within them over the persecution. Their minds were screaming – "Fight! Run! Just do something!" But the sad truth was they couldn't take on the Roman Empire or make the suffering, fear, and paranoia go away. Nor could they escape it. The known world was predominantly under Roman control so no matter where they would go – there Rome was also.

As a result, these early Christians became fearful, frustrated, and even angry. No doubt the pressure caused many of them to lay awake at night wondering when someone would come for them too. One can almost imagine the fear they are enduring, as their minds were telling them to "DO SOMETHING!" But there really wasn't anything they could do, as a result they were in danger of inescapably slipping toward hopelessness and despair.

CHAPTER 2

SHIFTING FOCUS

You might be thinking, What good does a shift in focus do? Seemingly, these people don't need an attitude adjustment, as much as a shift in political fortunes. But this is exactly what the apostle Peter seeks to do. Take a look: "Who have been chosen according to the foreknowledge of God the Father, set apart by the work of the Spirit, for obedience and for sprinkling with the blood of Jesus Christ. May grace and peace be multiplied to you" (1 Pet. 1:2, ESV).

Notice that word "peace" in verse two? It comes from the Greek "eirene" (eirene), which literally means a state of peace or freedom from anxiety. Another way to see it might be to recall that famous song from Bobby McFerrin, "Don't Worry Be Happy!" Now I know you are probably thinking, How could Peter possibly have expected them to have this abiding sense of overwhelming peace during all that was transpiring around them?"

He challenges them to peace and security. He does this by gently reaching out and cupping his reader's chins with his words, pointing them heavenward and shifting their focus from that which they are going to lose anyway to that which they can never lose. "Praise be to the God and Father of our Lord Jesus Christ! In His great mercy He has given us new birth into a living hope through the resurrection of Jesus Christ from the dead, and into an inheritance that can never perish, spoil or fade – kept in heaven for you" (1 Pet. 1:3-4, ESV).

Here Peter launches into a plethora of things the believer can never lose:

* Heaven in verse three;
*The Second Coming in verse seven;
*Salvation in verse nine;
*Our Savior, Jesus Christ, in verses eighteen, nineteen, and chapter two, verse four;
*The Word of God in verse twenty-three;
*Our election as children of God in chapter two verses nine and ten

These are all things the believer can never lose and the security for them is bound up in heaven. These dear Christians undergoing intense persecution and fear, and by extension us, have an ability to experience true peace and security because of the first few words of that second verse of 1 Peter 1: "who have been chosen by the fore-knowledge of God the Father." We are elect. (More about that later!) We have been chosen.

The point of this revelation is: if, as a child of God, you want real lasting peace, if you want the security of knowing your future is secure, you must recognize that these will only come when you set your focus and attention, on those things you cannot lose.

The apostle Paul also wrote about this same idea in his letter to the Colossians in chapter three, verse two (ESV): "Set your mind on things above, not on earthly things." Why would the apostle Paul tell Christians to set their minds on things above, on heaven? The answer is because Christians cannot lose things in heaven; however, they do, one day, stand to lose everything here on earth.

Many of us experienced the truth of this statement during the COVID-19 pandemic. Christians and non-Christians alike lost earthly things such as careers, houses, bank accounts, loved ones, and some even lost their own lives. Here's the deal: Because we all know that we can't take it with us when we die, if we spend our lives in the pursuit of those kinds of things, and the accumulation of more and more is what allows you to sleep at night; you are most assuredly setting yourself up for some major insecurity and anxiety.

Jesus told us in Matthew 6:25-34 that we shouldn't worry: not about life, what we'll eat or drink, not even about our bodies or what we'll wear. He said isn't life more than food and the body more than clothing? Then in Matthew 6:27 Jesus went on to ask a very pertinent question: "Can anyone add one thing to his life by worrying?" Of course, we know the answer to that is "no," but we still live, even as believers, as if we can!

Peter is teaching us that true security and peace is really a matter of our thought lives, that what we concentrate on is what we focus on. Imagine with me that our minds are like never-ending hard drives. And now imagine that your hard drive has recorded and catalogued everything you've ever done and every situation you've ever been in. This hard drive of yours enables you to play back these recordings on demand at a moment's notice.

What most people do is they access their hard drives and find files containing recordings of things they can and will lose; things they can't control and they play that file back in their minds. They play back video of a particular problem; or they go back over some conversation they've had and say, "Look at how so-and-so treated me." They review over and over some problem they've had with their bosses or spouses. They play back video in their minds of one predicament on top of another and, inevitably, the adrenaline begins to flow. Their blood pressure rises, feelings of insecurity begin to set in, and they begin to lose hope of any expectation of good in their future!

The apostle Peter is encouraging us not to do that. Instead, we are to place our chins into the words of 1 Peter and let them lift our focus from the here and now, from the things we can lose, to the things of heaven, to the things that are eternal that we can never lose. Consequently, we can then be filled with hope and encouragement that our future is secure.

CHAPTER 3

OUTSIDE OF TIME

I told you earlier about my failed attempt to take human anatomy in high school and how my desire to learn about the systems that allow us to function hasn't abated. If you knew me in high school, you'd know how crazy this next statement sounds...because it isn't just the human anatomy that interests me. I find myself now somewhat fascinated by the laws of physics and how they direct our world. I'm guessing that my fascination stems from the fact that everything we do on this planet (in fact everything anything does) is governed and restricted by the laws of physics. Things like Newton's Universal Law of Gravitational Forces – the law of gravity, or laws of force and motion, thermodynamics and even time. All these laws restrict and limit what we can do. Now, in the strictest sense, the laws themselves don't limit us but rather they reflect the natural laws put in place when the universe was created.

I promise this isn't going to be a college-level physics course but understanding some very basic things about the laws that govern our world can help us understand something precious about the nature of God and, thereby, encourage us when we find ourselves in seemingly impossible circumstances.

For example, on the one hand, the law of gravity is a physical law that restricts motion, both upwards and forward. We've all heard the saying, "What goes up – must come down." On another hand, the law of conservation of energy states that energy can neither be created nor destroyed – it can only be converted from one form to another. This means that a system always has the same amount of energy, unless it's added to from outside the system. This law is a part of the first law of thermodynamics. As a result we know that everything that expends or converts energy from one form to another, will eventually be exhausted of it's energy. In other words, the source of energy will eventually be depleted of it's energy.[15] For example, I have a friend in LaGrange, Georgia named Bret. He is an engineer who designs batteries for a worldwide battery manufacturer. No matter how well my friend designs and engineers those batteries, the amount of energy stored in them will one day be depleted. When that happens, my flashlight won't work because the batteries are dead. That's the first law of thermodynamics at work.

Another law that affects how we live is the law of time. Admittedly, this is one that is harder to wrap our minds around than most other laws of physics. However, this is the particular law I want us to grapple with in order to get a glimpse of the nature of God. In my simple mind, I break down the law of time this way – all of life is sequential. That is, one event follows another. You and I are restricted by the law of time. For us, life has to happen in a specific sequence. For example, we can't live or occupy the time known as Monday until we have passed through the time known as Sunday. We can't live in the time of May 11th, 2022 until we have lived through the time of May 10th 2022. That is, assuming you aren't born on May 11, 2022.

Imagine that I come through the rear door in the back of an auditorium. I can't exist in the time of standing in the front of a room until I have existed in the time and space of moving to that location. The law of time states that we have to live in the present. Once a time or a moment has passed, we cannot occupy that time ever again. For you and me, that time is gone forever. So, in spite of every Sci-fi story you've ever read, we cannot live or occupy the time known as the past nor can we occupy or live in the time known as the future. The law of time restricts us to living and occupying the time known as the present. We are locked into the present tense.

Now here's where it gets interesting. Unlike us, God is not restricted by the law of time. In fact, He is not restricted by ANY of the laws of physics. In other words, God is not restricted to the present tense and does not have to experience one day at a time. Instead, God lives outside of time. Isaiah 57:15 (ESV) says, "For thus says the One who is high and lifted up, who inhabits eternity, whose name is Holy." That passage tells us God inhabits eternity.

OK, but what does that mean exactly? Just this: God lives right now in the past, present, and future. For God, the past is not gone, nor is He waiting on the future to someday arrive. God doesn't sit up there in heaven and reminisce about the good old days. Nor is He waiting on next Friday like we do when we expect to get paid.

No, unlike us who are restricted by the law of time, for God, time is a constant! That means He sees Adam and Armageddon at once. He can see the creation of the universe and the events of Revelation at the same time. In Exodus 3, God declares that His name is "I AM." Even His very name speaks to His timelessness. God sees everything and dwells in every time – all at the same time. Past, present, and future are all the same to Him.

Here's the point: Once we understand God's perspective on time, that is He inhabits eternity, we can better understand the doctrines of election and predestination. In verse two of 1 Peter 1, the apostle Peter takes a theological deep dive and plunges us right into the nature and security of our salvation.

Back in verse one, we read, "Peter an Apostle of Jesus Christ to God's elect..." The first thing we need to understand is what this doctrine of election means. And to be honest, that word "elect" is an issue for many Christians. We don't like it; it's a hot button for denominations. But here it is in the text, and we need to deal with it honestly and in context.

To begin with, the word "elect" in verse 1 is translated from the compound Greek word "eklektos". Remember the New Testament in our Bible was originally written predominantly in the Greek language. So, we want to make sure that we understand the original meanings of words in order to understand the proper context for us. Eklektos is made of two Greek words: the prefix "ek" means out of and the root word "lego" (not a child's building block) means to select or choose. So "eklektos" means to select something out of or from a group.[16]

Now in the context of our passage here in 1 Peter, the Bible is stating that God has selected us as believers. For whatever His reasons, He choose us out of the general population of people occupying this world to be believers. I know this can be a hard thought to process, but this idea is permeated all throughout Scripture. Matthew 24:22, Acts 13:48, Romans 8:29, Ephesians 1:4, Colossians 3:12, and 2 Thessalonians 2:13 all speak to this subject.

God brought us to salvation before the foundation of the world. Before there was a universe, before Adam and Eve, before Noah or Moses or Abraham, God chose all those who were going to be saved. So, what does this mean to you? Just that if you are a Christian, you can lock your mind around this incredible truth: God chose you! All the way back in eternity past, you were a part of God's plan.

This would cause some to ask, "How can God be just if He only chooses some to be saved and not others?" I mean the Bible does say, "Whoever will may come." In John 3:16, we read: "For God so loved the world, that He gave His One and only Son, that whoever believes in Him shall not perish, but have eternal life." Romans 10:13 says, "For everyone who calls on the name of the Lord will be saved." So how do we rectify the thought that God chooses and we have a part in coming to Him as well? I think that answer is found right in our passage in 1 Peter 1:2 and we'll explore that next.

CHAPTER 4

FORESIGHT IS JUST LIKE HINDSIGHT...TO GOD

"...who have been chosen according to the foreknowledge of God the Father." 1 Peter 1:2 (NIV)

A quick recap might be helpful here. Verse one of our passage taught us that we are elect; that we were chosen before the foundation of the world. Verse two explained how that election to salvation takes place. The word "according" is what hitches the two thoughts together for us. We were chosen but it was according to God's foreknowledge.

According is translated from the Greek word "kata" (kata), which means "in accordance to" or "in agreement with." [17] It carries the idea of bringing or hitching two things or concepts together. Kata acts as a type of linguistic boxcar coupler. If you've ever watched an old western that features a train, you've probably seen a coupler. It's a mechanical device that connects two train cars together. Just like that mechanical coupler, "kata" hitches the two trains of our election and God's foreknowledge together. The point is God's election of those who would be saved has to be understood in light of His foreknowledge.

One of God's attributes is His foreknowledge. You may find this hard to believe but in a limited sense, we have this attribute available to us as well. You may be thinking that this is beginning to sound like all kinds of hocus pocus, but stick with me.

For instance, we can know the exact time the sun will rise tomorrow morning and the exact time it will set the day after. We can know the exact minute the apex of the high and low tides will occur. We can even determine the exact date of the next solar eclipse. We can know all these things with mathematical certainty BUT that doesn't mean we caused them to happen. In the same kind of way, but in absolute perfection, God knows everything that will ever transpire, and it is this foreknowledge, this ability, to know everything that influences His choice of election unto salvation.

The Bible translates it "prognosko". "Pro" means "before" and "gnosko" means "to know." We get words like diagnosis and prognosis from this root. So, putting them together, we find that "prognosko" means "to know before."[18]

Because God exists outside of time, that is the past, present and the future are all the same to Him. Because that is true, you can mark this down: God knows everything. He knows history before history becomes history.

Isaiah 49:9-10 (ESV) states it beautifully. "...for I am God, and there is no other; I am God, and there is none like me, declaring the end from the beginning and from ancient times things not yet done." God knows it all, even about you and me. God is saying He is different because He can stand at the beginning and describe the end. And we now understand that He does this because God has "prognosko"; He has foreknowledge. Remember from earlier that God inhabits eternity. He is not restricted by the laws of time like you and me. For God, events don't have to be experienced in sequence. God can exist in the "time" of Noah and Revelation simultaneously.

Here's what that means to us. Somewhere, sometime in eternity past, God looked down the eons of existence, and because of His foreknowledge, He knew that you would one day choose Him so He chose you. Now there are all kinds of implications here that because of space we can't get into. I know we aren't comprehensively covering this subject and I'm not presenting myself as having fully grasped all of it. But suffice it to say that God knew, even before you were born, you would choose Him, and because of this foreknowledge He chose you for salvation too. That's what verse two is referring to when it states, "...we have been chosen according to the foreknowledge of God."

You might ask, "Why does Peter dive right into such a deep theological subject right off the bat?" May I remind you to whom Peter is addressing this letter? These people to whom this letter first arrived were under intense persecution and hardship. They had been driven out from their own country, scattered like seeds across a field to other areas not their own. They were not welcome in these places. They were despised, hated, scorned, and even friendless. They began to lose jobs, homes, friends, and some were in fear of losing their lives. So, it was to these despairing and almost hopeless people that Peter pens his letter. And in so doing he gives them, and us, something to hold on to.

Firstly, he is reminding us that while we may not be the choice of this world, we are the choice of God. Therefore, be encouraged! Secondly, the apostle is forcing us to evaluate where we place our hope. He is helping us to discover that real hope, real peace, real life comes from placing our hope in things we cannot lose.

CHAPTER 5

WORTHY

O n September 11, 2001, the United States, and the world, was forever changed when nineteen hijackers took over four planes and left thousands dead and even more injured and scarred physically and emotionally.

Unbelievably, some of those who perished that day didn't die in the initial moments of the crashes. Some survived and were trapped in the upper floors of the Twin Towers, unable to escape. A not insignificant number chose to end their own lives by jumping from as high as 1,300 feet up. During their descent, their bodies would accelerate to a speed of about 150 miles per hour – not enough to black them out but fast enough to ensure death upon impact. [19]

I remember watching a 9/11 documentary by two French filmmaking brothers, Jules and Gedeon Naudet, and NY Firefighter James Hanlon. At one point in the film, one of the brothers is inside Tower One while the second plane strikes Tower Two. The fire chief is talking and in

31

the background, you can hear loud thuds just outside. The chief then exclaims something to the effect of "How excruciating it must be up there that people would choose to jump rather than hang on."[20] Those thuds were the sounds of people hitting the canopy awning covering the entrance to the building.

What happened that would cause these people to jump to certain death? What was going through their minds that allowed them to make this choice? I believe that it came down to the fact that they had widely lost any expectation of being rescued. They lost hope. Such a small word in the English language, but so powerful.

Edna Cintron survived the initial impact of the plane into her building. Her image is recorded by several cameras as she waves a white cloth from the hole left by the impact of the plane. She is pleading for someone to come rescue her, hoping beyond hope for someone to somehow make it to her. How was she able to hold out for so long when so many others did not? Simply put, I believe she had hope of rescue while others did not.

Emil Brunner, a noted Swiss Reformed Theologian of the last century, had a great analogy regarding hope. He said: "As oxygen is to the lungs, such is hope to the meaning of life."[21] It's been said that we can survive weeks without food, days without water, minutes without air, but we can't seemingly survive even one second without hope. If we lose hope, if we lose any expectation of good in our future, we can quickly be headed toward despair, depression, and insecurity.

Remember, the original recipients of this letter were in exactly that kind of situation. And to make matters worse, ordinary citizens were perpetrating much of the persecution they were enduring. Neighbors, co-workers, family, and even friends were administering much of the agony heaped upon these dear souls. And these Christians were in fear of losing everything. In terms of some type of expectation of good in their future – they didn't have any. So, Peter is seeking to encourage them to hold on. "Blessed be the God and Father of our Lord Jesus Christ! Who according to His great mercy has caused us to be born again to a living hope" 1 Pet. 1:3 (NIV).

Look at the first part of that verse. "Blessed be the God and Father." I want us to zoom in on that second word: "be." That word is not in the original Greek manuscripts. The original Greek doesn't say "Blessed be." Instead, it really says, "Bless the God and Father." Did you notice the not so-subtle difference between the two? The original isn't stating the fact "Praise be to God." Instead, it is issuing a command! "Praise God the Father."

That word "Bless," or maybe your version says "Praise," is translated "Eulogetos" and it means inherently worthy to be praised.[22] Here's the thing: In Scripture, this form is always ascribed to God because only God is inherently worthy to be praised.

Peter is telling these early Christians and us to offer praise to God, to bless His name. And we do that by reciting His attributes and the benefits of knowing Him. Look at Psalm 103:1-4 (NIV): "Praise the Lord, my soul; all my inmost being, praise His holy name. Praise the Lord, my soul, and forget not all his benefits— who forgives all your sins and heals all your diseases, who redeems your life from the pit and crowns you with love and compassion, who satisfies your desires with good things so that your youth is renewed like the eagle's."

We do this regardless of the fact we are facing incredibly difficult and painful circumstances because we are commanded to do so in 1 Peter 1, and because praising and blessing God lifts our spirits from the circumstantial around us to the heavenly above us. "Praise the God and Father of our Lord Jesus Christ, who according to His great mercy." 1 Peter 1:3 (ESV) That word "according" is the same one used in verse two and here it links praise to God and His mercy. God gives us this living hope because of His great mercy! Mercy was the motive behind God granting us eternal life. Mercy motivated God to reconcile us to Himself through the blood of Jesus on the cross. Ephesians 2:4-5 (ESV) says it wonderfully: "But God, being rich in mercy, because of the great love with which He loved us, even when we were dead in our trespasses, made us alive together with Christ."

One of the benefits of God's great mercy is "He has caused us to be born again into a living hope." 1 Peter 1:3 (NIV) That is cause for great praise! Living hope transfers us from the pain, suffering, and trials of this life to the realm of eternal life and hope in Christ Jesus. Eternal means it never ends.

Not only does our living hope never end, verse four of 1 Peter 1:4 says, "to an inheritance that is imperishable, undefiled, and unfading, kept in heaven for you." (ESV)

That's why our hope is living. That's why we can have an expectation of good in our future. We're going to dig further into the enduring nature of this living hope in the next few chapters, but I want to leave this chapter reminding you that the means or way to have this living hope is only found through the new birth of life in Jesus Christ.

If you have never trusted Jesus Christ as your personal Lord and Savior, then you currently reside in the realm of the dead and dying. To be sure you may be living here on earth but your spirit — that part of you that was intended to live forever — is dead. Scripture teaches us that when we repent, that is turn from our sin and self-directed life to trust Jesus as our Lord and Savior, then in that instant we are given new life. Our spirit is made alive, and we possess that living hope we've been talking about.

Look at verse three again: "Praise the God and Father of our Lord Jesus Christ, who according to His great mercy, He has caused us to be born again into a living hope through the resurrection of Jesus Christ from the dead." Born again is translated from one Greek word, "anagennao". The prefix "ana" means new and "gennao" means beget. So anagennao means to be regenerated or to be born again.[23] That's the source of our living hope. And we know it is sure and true because of the end of that verse, "Through the resurrection of Jesus Christ from the dead." The means of appropriating or getting this living hope is being born again and the power or proof that it is true is the resurrection of Jesus!

CHAPTER 6

TURNING OUR HEARTS
TOWARD HOME

When I was younger, I had the privilege of traveling all around the world, mostly on mission trips but sometimes for work and other times for pleasure. I've been to China, Canada, the Caribbean, Eastern Europe — Hungary, Yugoslavia (now broken up into several distinct countries), Romania, Russia, and even Kiev, Ukraine, where I was present in the central square as they voted to separate from the Soviet Union, and some places in Western Europe too.

I've always loved visiting new places and learning about new cultures. But one thing has always been true — I always loved coming home! I loved coming back to family and friends and familiar customs and surroundings. I loved getting back to my own normal routines, eating at my normal restaurants, and sleeping in my own bed.

This same thought permeates the book of 1 Peter. It really is an encouragement of sorts about going home.

In verse one we are called strangers in the world. Not because we are "strange" but because this isn't our home. The original language refers to a stranger as one who is a temporary resident, someone who resides in a place for a season but permanently resides elsewhere. Peter is reminding us that though we are here for a season, we have a permanent home elsewhere.

Look at verse three of that first chapter once again — "Praise be to the God and Father of our Lord Jesus Christ! In His great mercy He has given us new birth into a living hope through the resurrection of Jesus Christ from the dead, and into an inheritance that can never perish, spoil, or fade. This inheritance is kept in heaven for you..." 1 Pet. 3-4 (NIV).

Whatever else our hope is, it is an inheritance. An inheritance is something someone gives you or pledges to you at some point in the future. When they pledge it to you, you then become an heir to whatever it is they have pledged. It is pledged or given to you based upon the relationship you have with the person giving it. That's the idea in play here in 1 Peter. As children of God, we are heirs to an inheritance because of our relationship to God the Father.

Now before we go any further, I think we might need a reality check here. As God's children, most of us don't fully appreciate the immensity of all that entails. We don't grasp the reality of all that we are heirs to.

I was watching Disney's remake of The Lion King. In the film, there is a moment when Mufasa, the current king, is instructing his son Simba, the future king. They are looking out over the horizon and Mufasa states that their kingdom comprises all that the sun touches. Simba, just a cub at the time, cannot comprehend and appreciate all that statement entails. He has not yet lived enough life to fully understand what he is heir to.

That's kind of like us when we first come to Christ. Like a young Simba, we immediately become heirs to an inheritance from God the Father the moment we are born again. But because we are babes in our understanding and relationship with God, we don't grasp the significance of that inheritance.

Instead, the things this life has to offer distract us. Many times, we even throw tantrums when we don't get what we want, or life doesn't go as we plan. It's kind of like seeing a toddler opening presents. At first, they're intrigued by the shiny wrapping paper and then the toy itself captures their attention. But, come back thirty minutes later and you invariably find them playing with the box. They just need to grow up a little to learn to appreciate the gift more than the box it was wrapped in.

First Peter 2:2 (NIV) says, "Like newborn babies, crave pure spiritual milk, so that by it you may grow up in your salvation." If we want to grow and mature in our faith, we need to ingest God's Word into our lives on a regular basis. We must study it and work it out. And as we grow and mature in our faith, we begin to, little by little, come to understand the significance of our inheritance.

So, what's so special about our inheritance? What about it should make us crave it and give us confidence of some expectation of good? Chapter one, verse four gives us our answer — "...and into an inheritance that can never perish, spoil or fade" 1 Pet. 1:4 (NIV). Peter gives us three highly descriptive words that describe the enduring nature of our inheritance.

"Never perish" from a Greek word meaning "incorruptible." Doesn't wear out nor does it turn to waste; it's imperishable and completely opposite from this world. Everything in this world is made up of chemical compounds. One primary law of chemistry is that substances tend to break down into their most basic elements. For example, if you left a concrete block out in the elements, over time it would begin to crumble and fall apart. That's the nature of everything in our world. Age, heat, moisture, etc., all bring on and accelerate the process of decay. This happens with all kinds of things: houses, cars, clothes, you name it. We can be encouraged because this basic law of chemistry does not affect our inheritance from God; it will never perish.

Our inheritance will also never spoil. It is undefiled, unspoiled, free from contamination. Sin spoiled creation, resulting in tears, pain, sorrow, and fear. But our inheritance won't experience any of that. No sorrow. No tears. No pain.

And finally, our inheritance will never fade. In Paradise Lost, John Milton describes amaranth, an immortal flower that never withers or dies. It's a symbol of perpetuity. As Christians, our inheritance, like the amaranth flower, is unfading. It never withers, fades, or dies. In the world of our inheritance, our bodies will be immortal and incorruptible.

When I was growing up, both sets of my grandparents lived in Key West, Florida. We'd travel back each summer to visit and spend summer vacation. While there, we'd go to Smathers Beach to soak up some sun and play in the surf and sand. On one such visit to the beach, I decided to build a really cool sandcastle. At least for a kid my age, it was really cool. It had turrets, a moat, and multiple levels: everything a sandcastle should have according to an eight- or nine-year-old kid. Well, I eventually finished and stepped back to admire it, along with the thousands of enthralled beachgoers standing by to watch. (Ok, so there weren't really thousands but the few who did happen by commented favorably.)

As I was admiring my handiwork, I noticed that the water was getting closer and closer to my masterpiece. I thought I had built far enough up the beach for it to be out of danger from the waves. At first, the waves were no threat but as the day wore on and I was distracted with my creation, the waves were increasingly coming closer and closer. By the time we left for the day, the waves were right up on it. I came back the next day and there was nothing left but flat sand.

As I was reflecting on that memory, I realized that's exactly what life is like. We spend our lifetimes in pursuit of and building our castles and kingdoms. However, unbeknownst to us, the waves of death are ever inching closer and closer. At first, they seem almost imperceptible. Later on, we notice them now and then. And then one day, it seems as if they are lapping at our feet and the realization that they are inescapable dominates our thoughts.

Eventually the waves of death overtake us, and we fade from this life. Everything we've worked for, everything we've accumulated vanishes from sight for us.

Inevitably someone digs a hole in the ground and drops our casket in. If we're fortunate, some loved ones weep for a day and then, in time, we're forgotten. What a sad ending that would be if that's all there is! Thankfully for the child of God, we know that it isn't. We have a future that is bright! It is imperishable, unspoiled, and never fades. It's made up of the same material as eternity and is ours forever.

CHAPTER 7

RESERVED

B ack in 2005, my family and I moved from Palmetto Bay, Florida just south of Miami, to Peachtree City, Georgia, just south of Atlanta. I don't know if you've ever had to move, and odds are that you've had to at least once, but it is an incredibly stressful undertaking. There is the stress of getting things ready to move, downsizing, transferring schools for the children, finding a new place to live, hiring a realtor and selling your current home, learning the culture and customs of the new location, saying goodbye to friends and family, fear of making new friends and wondering if you'll ever fit in again, cleaning, packing, and transporting your things. It seems that the list goes on and on regarding everything you must know and get done each time you move.

Back to 2005... we moved in a whirlwind. It was the peak of the housing market just before the market crash. The Lord protected us, and we give Him all the credit! We interviewed a realtor but didn't sign a contract when one of our friends, actually someone more like a sister to my wife, knew a neighbor of hers who had an ex-sister-in-law who was looking to move into our neighborhood. Convoluted, I know! But three hours after meeting this woman and her husband, we had a signed contract on our house.

As we closed the door on that home for the last time and climbed into our vehicles to make the drive to Georgia, I realized that we weren't marking the end. Instead, we were making a transition from one location to another. While reflecting on this, I realized that is kind of what death is like for the child of God. When we die, it's as if we are pulling the door shut on this world but it's not the end. We are only moving from one location to another. We're simply moving to a new home in a new place.

"Praise the God and Father of our Lord Jesus Christ. In His great mercy He has given us new birth into a living hope" (1 Pet. 1:4, NIV). Look at that word, "hope." It's from the Greek word "elpis" and it literally means "a confident expectation of some good in the future."[24] As born-again children of God, we are heirs to an inheritance that will never perish, spoil, or fade. I don't know about you, but that sure seems like something that qualifies as a confident expectation of good in our future! Our inheritance of eternal life is not subject to the same laws of nature that govern how our universe, and everything in it, operates. And how do we know that it will never perish, spoil, or fade? Because the end of the verse is our guarantee: "...kept in heaven for you" (1 Pet. 1:4b, NIV). Our inheritance, the one that is never-ending and cannot spoil or fade away, is kept in heaven for us! And, dear Christian, who is the chief occupier of the place called heaven? It's God, right? That's who is keeping your inheritance from ever ending, spoiling, or fading. God Himself is the guarantor of your inheritance. That should give us all great confidence and expectation of good in our future!

Just like everyone else who has ever breathed, I'm not immune to the worries that come with living. Sometimes we are burdened and weighed down with all that life throws at us. I do believe it is immensely helpful if we can shift our focus from the burdens, trials, and problems of this life and instead focus on our inheritance — our eternal home and the strong promise God gives us in His Word regarding it.

You might be saying, "Well, James, that sounds good and all but how do I know it's true?" Let's go back and take a look at another word in that phrase. See the word "kept," or "maybe your version says "reserved." It translates from the Greek "tereo" and it means "to watch over, to guard diligently, to keep one's eyes fixed upon."[25] In our context, this means that our inheritance is being reserved or held for us. You know what a reservation is — it insures your place. You want to go to a nice restaurant (ok, pre-COVID), you make a reservation so they will hold a table for you at a particular time. You go on a business trip, and you make reservations for your air travel, your hotels, etc. Failing to do so could prove disastrous! In fact, one time back when my wife Cara and I were much younger, we used to take mini getaways to Disney World for a long weekend. Well, one time, several families had decided to take a trip and they all wanted to stay in the Disney campground, Fort Wilderness. The other families had pop-up campers and had done this before. We had never done this, as Cara isn't much of a camping kind of person. However, it just so happens that my parents owned an RV and since they didn't have any plans to use it that same weekend, they agreed to let us take it on the trip.

Fast forward to the getaway weekend and we're all caravanning to the resort. The other two families check-in with no problem and get their site assignments. However, the person checking me in can't seem to find our reservation. To add insult to injury, the resort is booked solid that weekend — no availability. I had called and spoken with a booking agent. I had ordered tickets for the theme parks. But somehow, I had not given my credit card information to reserve our spot in the campground. We were up a creek without any paddle! No reservation. It was as if I just showed up and expected them to have space available for me.

Just like my lack of a reservation at Walt Disney World, the Bible warns those who think that they'll be able to just show up one day and get a room in heaven. In Matthew 22:1-14, Jesus tells a parable of a king who was giving a wedding feast in honor of his son. All those who had been invited made excuses as to why they could not attend. Since the banquet was already prepared, he admonished his servants to go out into the streets and invite everyone they could find — whether good or bad.

The banquet hall was filled with guests. However, when the king came in, he noticed that one of the guests wasn't wearing a wedding robe. When the king asked why he wasn't properly dressed, the man had no answer. He was speechless. The king then told the attendants to bind the man's hand and foot and cast him out into the outer darkness. That man didn't have an answer because he thought he could make it on his merit. He didn't have a proper reservation.

Believer — your inheritance in heaven is already set! It's being kept, guarded over diligently, and watched intently by God Himself. If you are His child, there is absolutely no way that your inheritance isn't secure and your place assured.

CHAPTER 8

HOPE THROUGH TRIALS — PROTECTION

B ack in the late seventies and early eighties, Miami Southridge Senior High School, which I attended, had an award-winning choral program. I really couldn't sing a lick but my friends were in the program, so I joined up also. And believe it or not, back then it was a "cool thing" to be a part of something that had achieved such a level of excellence — even if the thing itself might not be considered cool.

Fast forward to one of our competitions being held in Orlando, Florida. We were staying at a resort and there were a lot of us there. Schools from all over the state were in attendance. Well, being teenagers there was no way any of us were going to stay in our rooms! So, a bunch of us decided to go check the resort out. There was probably upwards of about thirty-five to forty of us hanging out. The time came for us to get ready for our next performance, so about twenty-nine of us jumped into the first elevator that opened . Well, that's not really how it happened ... some of us got on and then more kids decided to pile in rather than wait for the next elevator. Needless to say, we were pressed in like sardines in a can! It was so jam-packed in there I wasn't even really able to lift my hands away from my sides.

As elevators are supposed to do, the doors closed, and we began our ascent to the upper floors where all of us were staying. However, something happened along the way. After about a minute or so, the elevator stopped moving altogether. And to top it off — the doors weren't opening because we were stopped between floors. Then to make matters even worse, after about two or three minutes of someone pressing the alarm button, ringing incessantly in our ears, we began to smell smoke in the cabin. The young girl next to me began screaming in fear and other voices began to be raised as people began to call for help. We were quickly descending into chaos inside the elevator car and in all the commotion and panic, our eyes and minds were cast downward, our thoughts turned inward, and uncertainty became our unwelcome companion.

Eventually, I was able to lift first one arm and then another over my head. I began to look for an access panel in the roof, hoping that I would be able to somehow climb out and up and go for help. Unfortunately, there was no hatch to the top of the car.

As I thought back to that episode in my life, I realized we're a lot like that when it comes to life, aren't we? As long as there is some light or ray of hope, then there's no dilemma that we can't see our way through. But take away that hope, block out the light, and the result is a hopeless grind. This is even true of you and me as children of God. As long as we keep our eyes and thoughts fixed on Jesus, there are seemingly no tight places we can't manage to work our way through. But block our vision of the "SON" light, distract our thoughts from the amazing hope of heaven, and our eyes begin to be cast downward and our thoughts turn inward and we begin to despair.

Back to my story... after about ten, maybe fifteen minutes, I hear these wonderful words from one of my fellow citizens in the elevator — "I hear someone!" At that instant, the mood in that elevator immediately changed. We went from near panic to exhilaration, from uncertainty to great joy! Listen, even though we were still in the same predicament, still stuck in an elevator with no way of escaping on our own, WE HAD HOPE!

Remember, this is the apostle Peter's theme to his audience. In fact, we've learned that, as children of God, we can have a confident expectation of good in our future.

At times, life can be like being stuck in an elevator — darkness, confusion, fear, uncertainty, all of which can incite us to despair and hopelessness. I know some of you reading these words are there right now. You are present tense filled with a pervasive sense of hopelessness. As I write these words, my wife and I are struggling to find the light at the end of the tunnel we are in. Just like you, we are weighed down, burdened, and broken by life. I know there are times when you just can't see any real hope of any good in your future.

But take heart! There is hope because God is present tense right there with you, guarding you and surrounding you with the resources of heaven to assure your inheritance.

Look at 1 Peter 1:5 (NIV): "who through faith are shielded by God's power." The apostle is showing a promise of God to us. See that word "shielded"? It's from a Greek word "phroureo". This is one of the strongest words available in the Greek language to convey this meaning. In fact, it is so strong of a word that I'm not convinced "shielded" does it justice. When I think of a shield, I normally think of something in front of someone or something. Shields I've seen don't cover much as they are meant to be wielded, to ward off the attack of an enemy.

This idea doesn't do justice to phroureo. This is a military term that literally means "to be garrisoned with troops, to be guarded by troops."[26] You are literally being (all the time) guarded by all the powers of God. God Himself, Jesus the SON, the Holy Spirit, and the armies of heaven are protecting you. To further encourage you, the present tense participle indicates continuous action. Basically, this passage says that you are always continually being protected, guarded, and garrisoned with all the powers of God!

So, the next question ought to be, "For how long is this true?" If you're like most people, you think that at some point you're supposed to be able to stand on your own, right? God certainly expects you to be able to handle things without His help. However, look again at verse five: "… who through faith are being (garrisoned) by

God's power until the coming salvation that is ready to be revealed in the last time." You and I are in God's protective custody until the last time, until the end of time itself. We're guarded and protected by all the powers of heaven until the time when Satan, demons, evil, and sin are no more! Until then, God is intently watching over us, protecting and keeping us secure in our salvation.

One time, I was flying from Miami, Florida to Moscow, Russia on a mission trip. Like every major airport in the country, Miami International Airport has a control tower, inside of which are people, whose sole responsibility is to ensure the safety of the planes and passengers in it's airspace. At the time, I knew several of these air traffic controllers and I trusted them with my life.

Our first stop was London, England. A storm was blowing across Europe, and we were landing in 90 mph winds. As an aside, I decided that day that I'm not sure the monitors on the planes that indicate airspeed, location, elevation, and wind speed of the plane are always helpful. The pilot, assured us that they were used to this weather and everything would be fine. We landed without incident and after a short layover, we begin the next leg of our trip to Vienna, Austria. As we were approaching the airport, the monitor was reporting 100+ mph winds. Again, we landed without incident and as we awaited our final departure to Moscow, we could see that the storm was rapidly blanketing off all visual markers and making it difficult to see outside of the airplane.

We finally departed for Moscow and by the time we arrived over the city, a massive fog had settled in.

Visibility was at zero! At this time, the Moscow airport was not rated for instrument-only landing beyond certain parameters. The pilot came on and explained this to us, then proceeded to share that we would circle for a while to see if the fog would lift and allow us to land. Otherwise, we would have to head back to Vienna.

This fog was so thick I could not see more than just a few feet outside of the airplane. I knew it was as bad for the pilot as it was for all of us passengers. However, he reassured us that while he certainly could not see out the front of the plane any better than we could, there was a man in a control tower at the Moscow airport who could see our plane and knew exactly what altitude and speed and heading we were on. He was watching and guarding our safety. In fact, in the end, the pilot, crew and air traffic control did such a good job, no one on the plane, outside of the flight crew, even knew that we were landing! The fog was so thick we had no point of reference, and the descent was so gentle that we had no perception of descending until we were on the ground!

That's how it is with God. No matter how dark or foggy our current circumstance may seem to us, He sees us. He knows your exact location, even if you don't see or feel Him. He is always and ever fixated on you, like active radar, even in your darkness. He knows your struggles, whatever they may be — family, financial, friends, job, whatever. He has you perfectly guarded by His power and will bring you safely home.

CHAPTER 9

HOPE THROUGH TRIALS — PURPOSE

In John 16:33 (NIV), Jesus says, "I have told you these things, so that in me you may have peace. In this world you will have trouble. But take heart! I have overcome the world."

Trials and tribulations are a part of life. They just come with the territory of living in the world. That word "troubles," from our passage above, carries the idea of pressure.

In the book of Romans, chapter twelve, verse two (ESV), we are told "... Do not be conformed to this world, but be transformed by the renewing of your mind." That verse carries the same idea of pressure. In everyday language, it's telling us not to let the world squeeze us into its mold of conformity.

So here we see Jesus is assuring us that we can expect troubles and trials as we go about our daily lives. However, He is also reassuring us that although we're going to experience trouble just like He did, we can also expect to conquer and overcome just like He overcame too. When He says for us to "take heart," that is exactly what He is inferring. He wants us to know that we have the same ability to persevere through trials as He did.

Romans 8:28 teaches us, "And we know that for those who love God all things work together for good, for those who are called according to His purpose." "All things" would also include troubles and difficulties. While that's great news, it still doesn't explain if our troubles have a purpose, and if so, what it is. To help us begin to answer this question, let's look at verse six of our passage: "In all this you greatly rejoice, though now for a little while you may have had to suffer grief in all kinds of trials" (1 Pet. 1:6, NIV).

To begin with, the apostle Peter tells us that we "greatly rejoice." The question becomes what is it exactly that we are to greatly rejoice in? In order to discover the answer to that question, we need to back up to verse five. "...who through faith are shielded by God's power ..." The apostle is relating our joy to our protected, eternal inheritance. That phrase "greatly rejoice" in verse six comes from a term that literally means to be exceedingly happy. And just for good measure, it is in the present tense.

This is conveying the idea of continual, ongoing happiness — not a happiness that is fleeting or temporary but a deep-rooted joy. So, no matter what our present circumstances, we know that our future, secured hope of heaven and the presence of the Holy Spirit within us allow us to greatly rejoice!

Here are a few thoughts about our troubles:

Troubles don't last — "a little while" — literally for a season. They will pass much as life does. In light of eternity, troubles are fleeting or momentary even.

Our troubles serve a purpose — they aren't just random acts that impact our lives. God can and does use them to do something to our faith! Sometimes they are meant to humble us or to break our desire for worldly things, to chasten us for sin and to strengthen our spiritual character.

Troubles bring distress — "grief" can refer to physical pain and mental anguish and sadness, sorrow and anxiety. By divine design, God uses distress and pain in our lives to refine us.

The apostle Peter penned this letter to these dear saints suffering intense and unrelenting persecution. However, unless he had gone through what he went through, he never would have been able to do it. Look at this story from the Gospel of Luke, chapter twenty-two.

As we pick up the story in Luke 22, we see an interesting development happening. Beginning in verse thirty-one, Luke 22:31-32 (NKJV): "And the Lord said, "Simon, Simon! Indeed, Satan has asked for you, that he may sift you as wheat. But I have prayed for you, that your faith should not fail; and when you have returned to Me, strengthen the brethren." The next recorded words spoken are from the apostle Peter. He declares that he is ready to follow Jesus whatever may come, prison or even death. His words carry such weight that the Gospel of Mark record of this story states that after Peter spoke these words, the others joined in agreement as well. The truly interesting thing is that here we have Jesus, God in the flesh, standing in a room with His disciples, knowing full well what is about to happen with and to them. God who is omnipotent, omnipresent, and omniscient knows that Peter will deny Him three times before the morning sunrise. If God is truly all these things, surely He knows Peter's heart and passion!

Yet, here we have a scene playing out where God does not intervene; at least not as we think He ought to have. Couldn't God have spared Peter this trial, this utter embarrassment, and this failure in his life? Instead, Jesus replies, "I have prayed for you, that your faith should not fail." Luke 22:32 (NKJV) Jesus certainly knows what will happen with Peter after the night's three denials: nevertheless, He allows the drama to play out to its final scene.

From reading the account, we all know that Peter did indeed deny Jesus three times that night. From further study, we see that this failure has such a profound impact on Peter that he leaves the disciples and goes back to being a fisherman. Yes, he did run with the apostle John to the empty tomb following the report of Mary Magdelene. He entered the tomb and saw the linen cloths and handkerchief lying there; in contrast, when John entered the tomb, he saw the same cloths and believed! No such statement of belief is attributed to Peter. After this, the Scripture tells us that they went away to their own homes. Did you catch that? Peter was not even found with the other disciples just a few days later. Peter was devastated by his failure. This is why we read in Mark 16:7, (NKJV), "But go, tell His disciples and Peter that He is going before you into Galilee."

Why would Jesus allow this to happen? The simple answer is God is infinitely more concerned with our "being" than with our doing. God knew, Jesus knew, and even the Holy Spirit knew that Peter had to endure this trial in order to become what he needed to become, in order to later do what he needed to do. If we turn to the discourse in the Gospel of John, beginning in chapter 21 and verses 15 and beyond, we see that Jesus is speaking to Peter. Three times Jesus asks him if he loves Him supremely. Peter responds that he loves Him but with a word that does not infer total devotion. The Peter we know from earlier times probably would have been so brash as to respond affirmatively.

However, the Peter we see here has been broken. His confidence is not what it was. He has failed Christ, miserably and publicly. On the third time, Jesus then uses the word Peter has been using as if to say, "Peter, do you even love Me only this much?" Jesus definitely knew that what Peter was going to do would require total devotion to Him. If Peter had not undergone this prolonged trial in his life, the likelihood is that he never would have developed the character traits necessary to lead the fledgling church through all its trials and tribulations during those first tenuous years.

If you don't think that this was an incredible accomplishment, take some time and read through early church history. Cultural wars between the Jews and Gentiles, persecution, false teachers, imprisonment, and death all were daily occurrences during the formative years of the early church. God knew that Peter had to "become" what he needed Him to become in order for him to do what He needed him to do.

The point for us in this illustration is that God may be shaping you, or even others around you, through troubles and hardships, just as He shaped Peter.

Additionally, we see in verse seven of our passage that trials and troubles also serve another purpose in the life of a believer. "These have come (what has come? Trials! Why?) so that the proven genuineness your faith - of greater worth than gold, which perishes even though refined by fire - may result in praise, glory and honor when Jesus Christ is revealed." That phrase "proven genuineness" comes from a judicial word in the Greek, "doikimion". It literally means to put something on trial to determine if it is true! [27] The implication is that God tests the believer's faith to test its genuineness. And by the way — God doesn't do this so that He can figure out who is a true believer. He does it so that true believers will gain confidence in their proven faith. Quite simply — one dramatic way to know the genuineness of your faith is how you handle trials... do they drive you away from Jesus and into bitterness, anger, and despair, or do they cause you to cling more tightly to Him for help in times of your trouble?

So, we learn that our trials do have a purpose, a divine one, in fact. God may just be shaping you for some further task, or He may be molding you into the likeness of Jesus to prepare you for heaven. Just know that you are not alone in your trials and troubles and that "all things work together for good to those who love God, to those who are called according to His purpose" (Romans 8:28, NKJV).

A few years ago, I was going through an incredibly difficult time in my life. I felt a sense of loss and confusion like I'd never felt before. I felt abandoned and needed to know that God was still with me. I needed to know that though I walked through the valley of the shadow of death — that God was guiding me, and that He'd not left me.

Several times during this period, I cried out to God for reassurance. And don't you know that in my darkest moments, when I absolutely couldn't take another step — when I was losing all sense of hope — He answered me! I'm here today because He answered me. I was and am still precious to Him. There was purpose in that trial in my life, and I greatly rejoice that He brought me through. But even more than the fact that He brought me through is the amazing thought that the trials and troubles will one day result in praise and honor when Christ returns! "These have come so that your faith of greater worth than gold which perishes even though refined by fire may be proved genuine and may result in praise, glory and honor when Jesus Christ is revealed" (1 Pet. 1:7, NIV).

Notice the sentence structure in that verse. It is not indicating that our trials give glory and honor to Christ (though they do); rather, it is indicating that at His appearing on earth again, we will receive glory, honor, and praise from Him because we were found faithful through our trials. I think it's one thing to think of praising Him for seeing me through so much difficulty; it's quite another to think of Him praising me! How awesome will that be to one day hear, "Well done, good and faithful servant." Matthew 25:23, (NKJV).

CHAPTER 10

GUARD YOUR MIND!

C ara and I have almost always owned trucks as our main means of transportation. We've owned Chevys, Fords, Dodges, and even a Mitsubishi Montero. One thing they all had, in fact ALL automobiles nowadays have in common, is something called the "BRAIN." The brain is a small computer tucked up somewhere underneath the dash and it controls most of the car's functions. Things like the fuel injection system, the electrical system, even some of the mechanical functions are governed by this brain.

This brain is so important to the functioning of the vehicle that if it failed, the car would be useless, unable to function as it should. Unfortunately, Cara and I learned this lesson firsthand. One day, the Montero began to stall out and then, eventually, the transmission began to lock up and not allow the truck to go into the proper gear. The electrical system started to misfire and then the real fun began when the mechanic told me it would be about $2K to replace it! But there's little you can do in that situation.

Without the repair, the automobile is unreliable, unfit for that which it was intended. To try and drive a car in such a condition is unwise and leaves you, and any other occupants of the vehicle, vulnerable and exposed to danger.

Now if you'll permit me, I'd like to draw an analogy to that vehicular brain. Situated inside your skull is an approximately 3 lb., jelly-like mass that sort of looks like crinkled Play-Doh®. It is actually the world's greatest "supercomputer" consisting of over 1 billion neuron connections. In terms of computing power, that 3 lb. Play Doh® looking substance is without equal.

Back in the sixties and early seventies, at the height of the Cold War with Russia, our family was stationed at Strategic Air Command headquarters in Omaha, Nebraska. SAC, as it was called, was the nerve center for our country's defenses. The B-52 bombers carrying the atomic weapons targeted at Russia and the Soviet Union were controlled from this base. My dad worked a significant distance underground on a massive computer. That computer, on which the fate of the world rested, doesn't even come close to the power, complexity, and sophistication of that 3 lb., crinkled, Play-Doh® inside your head!

Your brain is the control center of your body. It controls and governs everything about you. If it begins to misfire, it can have a catastrophic effect on your behavior, desires, motivations, will, compulsions, and even decisions. And make no mistake, if it becomes unreliable, it can leave you vulnerable to poor decisions, compromise, evil, and sin.

God knows that Satan knows the computer in your head controls everything about your behavior. God also knows that Satan and his fallen angels are incessantly trying to penetrate your mind. And He knows that if your mind is left unchecked, unguarded, and undisciplined, it is vulnerable to those attacks, which can often lead to moral and spiritual failure. Consequently, God calls us to shore up our minds and focus on the sure hope we have because of our faith in Jesus.

So, the question then becomes how are we supposed to guard our minds? How do we stay focused? We see the beginning of this answer in verse thirteen of 1 Peter 1.

"Therefore, prepare your minds for action..." Look at the word "therefore," "dio" in the Greek. Dio is a transitional word. Here, it is used to transition us from one mood of speech to another. Without getting too technical, let me explain. In the Greek language, verbs are said to be in either an indicative mood or an imperative mood. On the one hand, the indicative mood means you are stating or indicating a fact. "Bible Study helps me prepare." On the other hand, the imperative mood gives a command: "James, study your Bible!"

Here's the thing: Everything we've studied thus far, from verses one to twelve of 1 Peter 1 has been in the indicative mood. That is, these verses simply state facts. Peter has been disseminating facts about what we have as believers:

(2) We have been chosen;
(4) We have an inheritance;

(5) Through faith, we are shielded by God's power;
(6-9) We have hope during trials;
(10 - 12) We have salvation & the WOG.

Thus far, there have been no commands. Peter is not telling us to do anything. It's almost as if he is cataloging or listing the benefits of being born again. "Elect, living hope, inheritance, heaven, guarded, etc." But in verse thirteen, the mood of the language changes dramatically and the word "therefore" signals that change. We move from indicative to imperative; from statement of facts to statements of command! "Therefore" is kind of like saying based on all these things I have just told you that you have in Christ, based on all those facts, here is how God commands you to live! Here is what you are to do.

"Therefore, prepare your minds for action." The word "prepare" comes from a word that literally means to gird up. The command is for us to cinch up the loose ends of our minds. It's a graphic depiction of what God is commanding us to do.

In the first century, men were often dressed in long, flowing, ornamental-type robes. If a man needed to move quickly, he would gather up the loose ends of the robe and secure them with a belt or cord to keep from tripping on them and falling flat on his face. The first thing a Roman soldier did before heading into battle was put on his belt and tie up his robe so that its loose ends would not hinder his combat effectiveness. When he girded up his robe, it indicated that he was serious about preparing for the life and death of hand-to-hand combat. [28]

In terms of his recipients, and by extension us, Peter is saying, "Pull your thoughts together. Discipline your mind." Just like the Roman soldier diligently and meticulously prepared for battle, Christians are to "roll up the sleeves" of their minds. We are to take the initiative in preparing and protecting our minds from Satan's attacks.

Now, I am going to be very pointed here because I see so many of God's people exposing their minds to temptation, teasing it on purpose or just leaving it exposed, uncovered, and unprotected. The average Christian household in America looks, acts, and is run the same as any other household in the country. We use the same coarse language everyone else does and think nothing of it. We fudge on our expense accounts or taxes and think it is ok because "Well, everyone does it." We buy the same magazines — for the articles of course. We visit the same websites, look at the same images, ingest the same filth. We talk about people rather than caring about them. We buy and want more and newer things rather than being content and using our excess to show true hospitality. We justify our consumption by telling ourselves that we deserve it. We're jealous if our neighbor or friend or coworker gets the latest giant screen TV or car or has a nicer house. We watch the same TV shows, subscribe to the same channels.

Listen! You cannot expose your eyes and your mind to this stuff without it undermining your purity and convictions! You need to go home and imagine that cable hooked to your TV travels all the way down to hell — because that is where all that filth you are ingesting into your mind originates! You're probably thinking, "But, James, I don't watch the really bad stuff." Listen to me: Anyone can avoid the really bad stuff ... it's the subtle evil that undermines your faith and, by extension, your hope. The fact that some of you are thinking my last statement is ridiculous is proof of its veracity. You've already moved further along the scale than you know.

A man or a woman will excitedly flirt with someone other than their spouse. They will lay their mind and emotions out there in the open. Next thing they know Satan has seized that loose end and they wind up in sin.

In 1 Peter 5:8 scripture tells us that Satan prowls about like a roaring lion, seeking whom he may devour. You can't have an undisciplined mind and have loose thoughts running around in your head without expecting to get BODY-SLAMMED by the devil.

This is a call to guard our minds. This is a command from God to ensure we do not expose ourselves to the evils of this world. Some of you like to think that what you do won't hurt you or anyone else around you for that matter. That is a lie! Some of you like to tempt the sin to see how "strong" you are in resisting. Some like to blatantly and arrogantly pretend that the junk you are watching, reading, doing, and saying doesn't affect you. Understand this: If you find yourself continually going back to any of these things ... and you can't figure out why... It's because you love this thing (whatever it is) more than you love Jesus and the gospel! I know that that's a strong state-ment. But understand this: Satan is going to seize any opportunity to undermine you and ultimately corrupt your thoughts and your life. Cut it out! Cinch up your mind. Take captive every thought. Do not give any chance for temptation to take root!

But let me also add that this text also calls us to discernment. 1 Peter 1:13 calls us to prepare our minds for action and to be self-controlled." Some translations will say "be sober-minded." The translated word literally means "not to be intoxicated," don't be drunk. Metaphorically, it means to be circumspect, alert, discerning, to be able to make distinctions, be capable of separating right from wrong, truth from error, wisdom from foolishness. It means not getting caught up in the world's way of thinking. This idea is all-encompassing! It entails categorizing one's priorities and balancing one's life so as not to be subject to the controlling and corrupting influence of your sinful nature.

I have a friend in Virginia named Eric who is a really good realtor. If you ever find yourself in Chester, Virginia and in need of a house, you should look him up. Eric talks about having a "sniff detector" to determine if an idea or something smells funny. Same idea here... A person who is sober-minded and self-controlled is a person who has learned to think antithetically. To think antithetically is the opposite of being gullible. In other words, just because someone says something, writes something on the Internet, or states it as fact even, on social media, doesn't mean you should just embrace it without examining it, (even this book). We hear this kind of stuff all the time from our news media or politicians.

God is calling you to learn to think critically, to evaluate things against His Word. Unfortunately, I'm afraid that Christians listen to Oprah, The View, Facebook or some news anchor more than they do to the Word of God! Pop psychology and worldly relativistic thinking have not only encroached on the church, but the church has also embraced them with open arms. In the name of political correctness, truth, or even the idea that there is such a thing as absolute truth is discarded and sacrificed on the altar in favor of being Facebook-liked and accepted by the culture around them.

If we don't begin to diligently guard our minds and cinch up our loose thoughts, we expose ourselves to Satan and put ourselves in danger of evil, sin, and despair.

CHAPTER 11

GOD IS GREAT. GOD IS GOOD... YOU'RE NOT GOD

Since we've encountered the pandemic known as COVID-19, many of the things we used to do have gone by the wayside. One of those that have always been dear to me is the idea of going out to eat at restaurants. Now I'm not talking anything fancy, per se; just a place to go and enjoy a decent meal and hang out with family and friends.

One of the places I used to like to go to eat occasionally was Golden Corral. Now before you jump all over me, understand that I enjoyed the variety. To be sure, I probably over-indulged whenever I would go there but hopefully not too much. However, I really enjoyed the ability to just get a little bit of whatever struck my fancy at the moment.

One time, as I was going through the line and watching the people ahead of me making their selections, I thought what an apt picture of our culture today. See, most people go to Golden Corral not because it's the least expensive place to eat; it's not. Nor do they go there because it's so exclusive and the food is the best. It isn't. No, people go to Golden Corral because they can create their own tailor-made meal from all of the choices in front of them. And just like those people in the restaurant, people in our society are big on having choices. To be honest, we all like options and dislike absolutes, don't we?

And the thought that really gripped me that day, and continues to occupy a place in my thoughts now, is that the process of creating your own meal at a buffet like Golden Corral is exactly like what people do today with religion.

Our society is not only big on creating their own customized meals at restaurants, we're also big on choice, individualization, and customization in every aspect of our lives, including our gods! We don't want to just have our food our way. We also want to have God our way too! We want a tailor-made God to suit our desires. We want a combination plate God who will endorse our lifestyle choices! And we'll embrace anything that helps us get that and feel better about our lives.

I read somewhere along the way that "God created man in His own image... and man has returned the favor." And just like the restaurant line — you can decide how you want to live, what you want to live like, and then you can create your own customized god that will endorse your choices. No harm, no foul that way. No guilt, since your god always understands because he/she/they is exactly how you want them to be.

This isn't much different then what we see played out on social media. For all the language back and forth about any particular subject, no one changes his or her mind! I read some of the comments and wonder if that person's mother knows how they're behaving... We want to act as if we embrace diversity and want people to express their opinions until it crosses paths with our own opinion or deeply held beliefs. We love picking and choosing from all the available choices and making a hodge-podge belief system that suits us.

The Bible has something to say about the nature of God. And we would do well to take heed. Unfortunately, many Christians and the churches they attend take liberties with God's character, attributing to Him all kinds of self-indulgent attributes. They adjust the nature of God in their minds and theology in order to accommodate their own likes and dislikes and, by default, sin.

"As obedient children, do not be conformed to the passions of your former ignorance." (1 Peter 1:14 ESV). Peter is literally calling his readers "children of obedience." The inference here is that obedience should characterize every child of God. This thought distinguishes Christians from non-Christians because non-Christians are called "sons of disobedience" (Col. 3:6; Eph. 5:6)

I want to make one thing absolutely clear: Obedience has not, nor will it, ever produce a believer in Jesus. However, a true belief in Jesus Christ will always produce obedience in the life of a Christian.

The emphasis in verse fourteen helps us to see that this call to obedience does not begin with outward actions, as much as it begins with our attitudes and mindsets. Peter is emphasizing that the way we comport ourselves will change only as the result of a natural outworking of an inner change. Have you ever heard the expression, "Garbage in, garbage out"? It was originally used of programmers writing computer code. If the code was junk, then junk is all you should expect to get from the computer. Just like that, when we put garbage into our lives, why should we expect that "everything will come up roses"? We desperately need to get the garbage out of our lives and begin to live as we say we believe!

The question then becomes, "If I'm truly saved, why do I still sin if my character is supposedly marked by obedience?" The simple answer is that Christians are sometimes marked by disobedience because, while their spirits are already redeemed, they are not yet sanctified. From the moment we become Christians, we are in the process of being made into the image of Jesus. This process continues until we are home with Him in heaven. Until then, we're all subject to, but not compelled by, our earthly natures.

This fact does not give one the freedom to live as one wants by embracing a life of sin. In fact, we read earlier that in Romans 12:1-2, we are told not to conform to the evil desires we used to have before we were saved. This means our lives should not be marked by these desires. We are not to be enslaved to them. In the last chapter, we learned that we love that "thing," whatever it is, more than we love our relationship with Jesus. We love the "thing" more than the salvation He has provided. We love the "thing" more than the assurance of heaven and our hope of the future. Instead, we are to be "obedient children." And in 1 Peter 1 look at what we're supposed to be obedient to. (15) "But just as He who called you is holy, so be holy in all you do." (16) "For it is written: 'Be holy, because I am holy.'"

Stop right there for a second. Remember we learned that Greek verbs are written in moods. We found the indicative mood signifies a statement of fact and the imperative mood gives a command.

Now with that in mind, take another look at vs. fifteen. "But just as He who called you is holy." The verb "is" is in the indicative mood. Meaning what? That this is a statement of fact. GOD IS HOLY! I don't know any of us who would argue against that fact. What exactly does that mean? I mean I say God is holy, and I'm sure that all kinds of thoughts begin to run through our minds. We think of organ pipes, stained-glass windows, religious men in robes speaking in Latin, incense, crucifixes, and cathedrals or some lonely guy sitting atop a mountain? Nothing could be further from the truth of God.

That word "holy" means different, separate, set apart. Distinct.

GOD is different from the world around us.

- The world loves its sin — God hates sin.
- World tolerates evil — God is intolerant of it.
- World sees relativism — God sees absolutes!

God always seeks to place distance between Himself and evil.

But we live in the "Age of Tolerance." We live in a time of compromise. Absolute standards of good and bad, right and wrong are absolutely rejected. Today, nothing is absolute except our belief that nothing is absolute. What's good is seen as what's good for me and maybe my family in any given situation.

The first time I experienced this happened many years ago. Among other responsibilities, I was in charge of our media team at my church. I came up with the great idea of broadcasting our services over this new thing called the Internet. (I told you this was many years ago!) Problem was the technology wasn't quite up to speed yet. These were the days of AOL dial-up and 56k modems! The systems in place simply could not handle the transmission speed and data needed to make video work over the Internet. However, I met a gentleman who thought he would be able to make it work. So, we purchased the necessary pieces of equipment and installed them in his place of business so that he could test his ideas and eventually we would be able to broadcast our services.

Fast forward about a year and we have made absolutely no progress. So, I approach this gentleman and request to get our equipment back and try ourselves. (I do have a degree in television and radio production after all.) Get this! He refused to return the equipment. Turns out he was using it for his own business and removing it would've caused a hiccup in his business plan. After repeated attempts to make an appointment to retrieve the equipment, I decided to show up at his place of business unannounced. During our ensuing conversation, something he said absolutely shocked me! He told me that he wasn't going to return the equipment because it wouldn't be good for him to do so. And he went on to explain that he believed that what was good for he and his family was "morally" good, regardless of how it impacted anyone else.

Words were exchanged and I said something just as shocking back to him (no, I didn't curse...) and after a conversation with his attorney, he agreed to give me back the equipment. I had never encountered such a thought process before.

And make no mistake — this isn't just the thinking in our culture; in many ways, this has become the thinking of Christians and the church! It's as if the world is infected with the idea of compromise and the church has caught the disease. See, the question for the modern Christian and church in America isn't "What does the Bible have to say?" No, the question has become "What feels best to me?"

Theology has been usurped by psychology. The pursuit of truth has been replaced by the pursuit of happiness. Sin is no longer the enemy of the church and the Christian; instead, sadness is. To help people feel good about themselves has become the #1 priority. So now even the church wants nothing to do with a Holy God who calls His people to be holy. We've toned down the holiness of God, adjusted His righteousness in our minds so that we don't have to aim or strive for holiness anymore.

The new trend in our churches today is to aim our lives at whatever we desire to live like and then "paint" our understanding of God around the arrow of our desire! Adultery, pornography, drunkenness, lust, greed, covetousness, selfishness, immorality, pride. These are no problem in our churches today not because they don't exist, but because they are tolerated and accepted as normal. Because "Hey, it's about what I believe, right?" We believe that as long as we are sincere, God is ok with it. Nobody's perfect, right? "So, God can't possibly expect me to be either" is the way the thought process goes.

So, we attempt to adjust God downward to accommodate our sinfulness. "I mean obviously if God didn't want me to enjoy these things, He wouldn't have made them so accessible and they wouldn't make me "feel so good. God doesn't want things to be difficult, right? He wants me to be happy!" We practice pain avoidance, believing that we don't deserve to experience any pain or trauma or difficulty of any sort.

Take another look at vs. fifteen (NIV): "But just as He who called you is holy." That's a fact. God is holy. We need to stop trying to adjust Him down to our sin and begin to adjust our lives up to Him. "But just as He who called you is holy, so be holy in all that you do. For it is written: 'Be holy because I am holy.'" (1 Peter 1:15)

God says, "I am holy. I seek to separate Myself from sin and that is exactly what I want My children to do as well." By the way, that phrase "Be holy" in vs. sixteen is an imperative in the Greek, meaning:

1. It is a command!
2. Not a suggestion.

3. Not an option to be chosen or set aside (No boxes to choose between.)
4. This is an order from a holy God to His people.

As born-again children of God, children of an inheritance, kept in heaven, reserved... We are charged to be holy, to be unique from the world around us.

o   The world lives to fulfill its own desires.
o   We are to seek to fulfill the desires of God.
o   The world lives by pop psychology wisdom, whatever sounds right.
o   We are to live by the wisdom of the Word of God.
o   The world is guided and enslaved to the desires of its flesh.
o   We are to be guided to seek to be self-controlled under the guidance of the Holy Spirit.

Why are we to be different? Look at 1 Peter 1 verse seventeen: "Since you call on a Father who judges each man's work impartially, live as strangers here in reverent fear." That phrase "reverent fear" has been terribly misunderstood by many. Some would believe that this is referring to the fear of God's discipline. However, the feel of this chapter seems to suggest a different understanding entirely. I believe that the expression doesn't so much reference a fear of God's judgment as it infers developing a "reverential awe" of God.

We are told, "Since we call on a Father..." the very fact that we are told to call God "Father" indicates that we are not talking about discipline for discipline's sake. Rather, it's implying a relationship, much like a child would develop toward a loving parent. The idea here is that we would want to please God and avoid anything that would grieve Him because we are so in awe of His greatness and holiness. "As obedient children, do not be conformed to the passions of your former ignorance." (1 Peter 1:14 ESV) Notice God did not say, "as soon as you are mature enough...."; or "When you finally get this garbage out of your system..."; or "When you think you are strong enough..."; or "When you have sunk as low as you possibly can and have nowhere else to turn." NO! God says cut it out! Stop being conformed to the evil desires, to your own selfishness, to your sin and depravity — Stop acting like you did before you knew better. You have a future, a hope reserved in heaven for you. You have been chosen, you have been saved, are being saved, and will be saved at Christ's return. Therefore, fix your hope, focus your mind, take captive every thought, and think on that and be encouraged! You have the Holy Spirit living inside of you and you can be holy!

The scheme of Satan involves dragging us down with the sins of this world and holding us captive to our failings so that we lose our distinctness in Christ. Consequently, we look, act, talk, lust, steal, murder, lie, cheat, and covet just like we did before we were saved and just like the lost world around us does. Why? Because Satan knows that our power to affect the world:

o   Does not come by being like the world;

o   But by our being different from it.

We impact this world for Christ not by being like it but by staying different. Lost people were attracted to Jesus precisely because He was different! He wasn't like the Pharisees. He wasn't like themselves either. Satan knows that the minute we lose our distinctiveness — we lose all impact and influence. That's why vs. fourteen tells us not to conform! Conformity is the opposite of holiness!

But how do so many of us live? We don't want to be too distinct. We don't want to be too unique. People might think we are weird if we are too different from them. So, what we try to do is straddle the fence. We try to bring God down to our level of comfortableness and along the way, we compromise our souls and spirits. "See I'm not that far from GOD, I can still see Him. I'm still close." But what happens is that the world keeps moving the line. Things we never thought possible morally last year, last month, and last week even, are now accepted as commonplace and "normal."

And as the Christian seeks to continue that middle ground, he or she has to keep compromising and moving farther and farther over to stay in the middle. Eventually, as he or she keeps moving over, they find that they have lost their distinctiveness and they are no longer attractive to the world. And even worse, they lose their desire to be, finding instead that they like this newfound freedom to choose how they want God to behave. It's kind of like a nail and a magnet. If the lost world is the nail and Christ in us is the magnet, the closer we get the more attractive we are.

But what happens when you put two magnets together? They repel each other. So, it is with us. Lost people don't want someone just like themselves. They want someone unique — someone different who can show them what they are looking for. They're looking for someone who has been changed by an encounter with Christ.

You want to find balance in seemingly impossible circumstances? Stay focused to the end! Fix your minds on your confident expectation of good in your future because of the salvation we have in Christ, and you can live according to your basic character... holy and distinct.

CHAPTER 12

THE SECRET INGREDIENT

I don't know if you can remember back to when you were in school... but if you do, you might remember those kids who just seemed to always get the top grades and never even seemed to try. Then there were the other kids who also did really well, but they struggled for their A's & B's.

I was kind of a hybrid of those two. Earlier on, middle and high school I breezed through. Never seemed to do any homework or much if any of the reading, but I always came away with decent grades. But at some point, probably around my first year of college when I took my first accounting class, things changed dramatically for me. All of a sudden, some classes were challenging, while in others I was seemingly able to coast along.

Fast forward a few years and I'm in seminary studying for the ministry. And honestly, I am absorbing everything I can, but the standards are set much higher and I'm working hard for every grade I get. Understand also,

Cara and I are in a different place financially than we had been previously. Before this time, I was the one who was always helping everyone else. Now, I was at a point where I can't afford the cost of going to school and I was having to ask for help almost every semester. That help came in the form of my former church stepping up and paying a significant portion of my tuition each year. Without their help, I'd never have been able to finish.

Well, I had a close friend in seminary by the name of Tom. Tom has since gone on to complete his doctorate and is helping people and doing tremendous work through his counseling ministry. We were in several classes together and consequently were assigned a group project together. In the midst of this project, Tom asked me why I studied so intently. Why do I work so hard to assure that I get an A? The implication behind the question was that maybe I was being prideful about wanting straight A's. And if so, that would conflict with the values we espoused as Christians and potential leaders of God's people. In other words, he was checking my motivation. I don't believe he was being mean. He was, and is, my friend and I care about him dearly. It was at that point that I explained to him how I was able to be in school in the first place. That if it weren't for the gracious support of some people at the church where I was saved, I wouldn't be able to afford seminary, studying for a life in the ministry. I further explained that every semester I sent back a letter and a copy of my grades to that church, thanking them for their support and promising to continue to try and do my best to be the best servant of the gospel I could become.

You see, it wasn't pride that motivated me, though I did want to do well academically. No, it was out of a grateful heart that compelled me to do well for all that had been sacrificed on my behalf. Their sacrifice allowed me to concentrate on my studies by keeping me from having to work two jobs and try to go to school at the same time.

I want to pause here and interject a thought. During our last couple of chapters, we saw how the apostle Peter had been calling for excellence in the Christian life! In fact, he had issued six commands for the people of God.

Beginning in verse thirteen:

1) Gird up the loose ends of your mind
2) Be self-controlled
3) Set your hope fully on the grace to be given you when Jesus Christ is revealed.
4) As obedient children, do not conform to the evil desires you had when you lived in ignorance.
5) But just as He who called you is holy, so be holy in all you do. For it is written, "BE HOLY, for I am holy."
   And the sixth one, which we did not cover but nonetheless is right there in Scripture.
6) Since you call on a Father who judges each man's work impartially, LIVE YOUR LIVES AS STRANGERS IN REVERENT FEAR.

Six commands! Six imperatives are given to the child of God. The bottom line of all six commands? Strive to live a godly life! Reach for excellence in service to Christ! But as we come to verse eighteen, the Word of God shifts gears, as it were, and reveals the motive for this call to godly living.

In verses thirteen to seventeen, the apostle has been calling us to excellence in our walk with Christ, but in verses eighteen to twenty-one, we discover the motive for this pursuit of excellence. The great motivational force we should be responding to as we seek to live a life of excellence for God is an ATTITUDE of GRATITUDE... thankfulness! That is the secret ingredient to the special sauce of finding stability in impossible circumstances.

Well, that begs the question, just what is it that we should be all that thankful for? Look at verse eighteen to find out, beginning with "For you know..."

Peter says you know something. He's declaring that as a child of God, you have a knowledge of something... and that knowledge of something is what should evoke thankfulness and gratitude in your life, regardless of your circumstances. And just for good measure, remember to whom it is the apostle is writing this little letter. People who, because of their faith in Jesus, were on the verge of losing everything — jobs, houses, country, family, fortunes, even potentially their very own lives!

I would never downplay anything any of us is ever going through. Truth is, whatever you are going through is tough for you because it's affecting you. I get it! However, none of us has probably had to endure the kinds of persecution and fear and trepidation that these dear brothers and sisters in Christ had to undergo. (To be sure, I do understand that persecution does still happen today across the world. However, as westerners, we have probably not had to endure this same type of hardship.) If he can ask this of them, then surely the Word of God here is applying to us as well.

Two things impact our ability to be thankful in various circumstances:

> "For you know that it was not with perishable things such as silver or gold that you were redeemed" (1 Peter 1:18 NIV).

The word "redeemed" in verse eighteen is translated from the Greek word "Lutroo" and it means to secure the release of someone or something through the payment of some type of ransom; by paying a price for the release of someone.[29] The word was used in the context of a slave being released from slavery for the payment of a fee and of a prisoner being released from prison by the payment of some price.

That's the idea here! See the whole drama of redemption in the Word of God revolves around the fact that mankind is enslaved to sin. Mankind is a prisoner to sin in this life and will ultimately be a prisoner to sin forever in hell! Those are the facts under which we live. But the entire account of Scripture, from Genesis all the way to Revelation, is that God would pay a price... a ransom that would make it possible for man to be released from the grip of sin, death, and hell. The Bible is, among other things, a book about the redemption of the human race.

But what would be that price? What price would have to be paid in order to redeem man's soul? Well as we've just seen in our passage, Peter begins by telling us what the price was not!

"For you know that it was not with perishable things such as silver or gold that you were redeemed." (1 Peter 1:18 NIV) Translation: Money won't save your soul from hell! The payment of money to God, no matter how much, will not extract your soul from hell's grasp. So, take all the money from Elon Musk, Warren Buffet, Bill Gates, and Jeff Bezos, and you still don't have even enough to make a down payment on saving just one soul!

In verse 18 of 1 Peter 1 Peter says, "You know". There are two words in the Greek language translated as "know." The most commonly used of the two is "gnoskis". Gnoskis means intellectual knowledge, but that's not the word used in verse eighteen. No, the word in verse eighteen is "oida" (oida). It refers to elementary or basic knowledge. [30] Peter is saying, "I'm telling you something that you already know. This is basic stuff."

But what was it they already knew? What was this elementary knowledge? "For you know that is was not with perishable things such as silver or gold that you were redeemed..." (1 Peter 1:18 NIV) He's saying just with a casual knowledge of Scripture, you know that you can't be saved with money. That's basic; that's a given.

Yet, we know that today there are still people who think that everyone and everything has a price, even God! There are false religions that openly teach that God and heaven can be purchased, that judgment can be escaped with the right amount of money.

Here's what Scripture says about that. Isaiah 52:3: "For this is what the Lord says: You were sold for nothing, and without money you shall be redeemed."

It reminds me of a story I heard about some scientists who challenged God because they said they had discovered the ability to create life. So, God accepted their challenge. The appointed day and time arrived for them to square off, and the scientists begin to gather their elements. One of them grabbed a shovel in order to scoop up some soil when God quickly interjected, "No, get your own dirt!" To somehow imply that you can pay God money to redeem your soul flies in the face of His holiness! Who do we think we are that we can buy God off, especially with things He created in the first place?

Look with me at Psalm 49:7 (NKJV): "...those who trust in their wealth and boast in the multitude of their riches, none of them, can by any means, redeem his brother, nor give to God a ransom for him." What's the point? Just this: You can't buy redemption! You cannot purchase salvation, nor can you purchase someone else's!

Any religious system that seeks to tell you differently needs to be avoided at all costs! All the gold, all the silver, all the precious metals, all the currency, the composite wealth of everyone for all time would not be enough to pay the price of redeeming even one soul! To think that money would be sufficient payment to God is an affront to Him. That thought flies in the face of the sacrifice of Jesus on the cross! You say, "James, if money wasn't the commodity that God ordained to save us, then what was?" What was the price? How did He redeem us?

"But with the precious blood of Christ" (1 Peter 1:19 NIV) Only one thing redeems us from our lives of damnation, and that is the sacrifice of Jesus' blood on the cross. To be sure, all blood is special because it sustains life. But the blood of Jesus is even more special because it gives eternal life and saves us from eternal death.

I know this isn't a science book, but I thought this next section might be germane to our study. I think there are some parallels between our blood and the spiritual power of the blood of Christ that we should explore.

Within the human body, there are many different types of tissues: muscle, nerve, fat, bone, epithelial, connective. These tissues all have one thing in common: They are all fixed; they are stationary. That is, they're restricted to one place in the body. However, there is one tissue that is not fixed in place. It is fluid, mobile, and moves all throughout the entire body. And as it travels, it comes in contact with all the fixed cells from all the other tissues In so doing, it supplies them with vital nourishment so that you can live.

This tissue is called the blood. And it consists of a colorless liquid called plasma in which are suspended a number of elements. The solid part of blood consists of platelets, red cells, and white cells. Red cells contain a mysterious substance called hemoglobin. Hemoglobin is an iron compound that has an attraction to oxygen. By the way, oxygen is the fuel of your body. These red cells travel through the body, through the lungs, and there they unite with oxygen to form oxy-hemoglobin.

In this form, they travel to all the fixed cells in your body and deliver oxygen. Then this same red cell picks up the waste product from the fixed cell, CO2, cellular garbage, and delivers it to the bowels, kidneys, sweat glands, etc. Your red blood cells are literally a delivery man and garbage man all in one!

What a picture of the blood of Jesus Christ... His blood provides us with the nourishment of eternal life and, at the same time, cleanses us from the garbage of sin. In fact, 1 John 1:7 (NIV) states, "And the blood of Jesus cleanses us from all sin."

Ok, that's the red blood cells; about five million per cubic millimeter. The white cells only number around 5,000 per cubic millimeter. But that number can change dramatically, rapidly even. Those 5,000 cells per cubic millimeter are really your body's "peacetime" army. But when an infection occurs, and your body is attacked by enemy germs, instantly the number of white blood cells is multiplied and this army rushes to the point of infection.

For example — have you ever cut your finger and witnessed an infection begin? Your finger begins to swell up? This is due to blood being rushed to the scene of the infection or injury. And the white cells in that blood begin to lay siege to that infection. They declare war on those infectious germs. Incidentally, millions of these white blood cell soldiers are killed in the battle. They give of their lives to save the physical body.

What a graphic picture of the blood of Jesus Christ whose blood was shed in death and who saved us from the infection of sin. And please don't misunderstand me; I don't pretend to know much of anything, let alone everything, about human blood... nor do I presuppose to call myself an expert on the blood of Christ... but I do know this. In 1876, Robert Lowery was right:

What can wash away my sin? Nothing but the
blood of Jesus;
What can make me whole again? Nothing but the
blood of Jesus.

Refrain: Oh! precious is the flow That makes me
white as snow;
No other fount I know, Nothing but the blood of Jesus.

For my pardon, this I see, Nothing but the
blood of Jesus;
For my cleansing this my plea, Nothing but the
blood of Jesus.

Nothing can for sin atone, Nothing but the
blood of Jesus;
Naught of good that I have done, Nothing but the blood
of Jesus. [31]

Friends, the price was high to save you and me, and all the world, from the effects of sin... It should inspire us to live lives full of gratefulness and thankfulness for all He has done

CHAPTER 13

LEARNING TO LOVE LIFE

A little over thirty years ago, a song was released that captivated the world's attention. People everywhere were singing it and humming its tune, even adopting its message as a way of life.

The really cool thing about this song, and what made it become such a hit, is that there were no instruments used in the recording of the song. That's right; the entire song is made up of instrumental sounds made up entirely by utilizing just the artist's voice.

But it's the words of the song that really captured people's attention and changed their lives. While the message of the song was quite simple, it was nevertheless quite compelling also.

The singer, Bobby McFerrin. The song: "Don't Worry Be Happy" Here's a sample from it:

> "Here's a little song I wrote, might want to
> sing it note for note — don't worry, be happy!

EVERY life will have some trouble, when you worry, you make it double —don't worry, be happy. Don't worry, be happy now!

When you worry, your face will frown. And that will bring everybody down! Don't worry, be happy.[32]

Simple message really... but profound! Trouble is to be expected in this life but being happy is a choice. In other words, being happy is a discipline of the mind!

This isn't a new paradigm. Almost 2,000 years ago, the apostle Peter proposed the same thing in the little letter we know as 1 Peter, specifically in chapter three. He is talking to Christians about learning to love life, as opposed to hating it. He is teaching his readers, and by extension us, how to see good days as opposed to miserable days. He's giving us instructions regarding how to be happy regardless of life's circumstances. So, the question becomes how do we learn to love life; how do we come to view our days as being good?

Beginning in verse eight, we come to a new theme that continues all the way to verse twelve. And the theme is summed up in verse ten: "For whoever would love life and see good days." (1 Pet. 3:10, NIV).

You may be thinking "Why is he talking about loving life and seeing good days? I would suppose that we all desire to love life and we all desire for our days to be good. Isn't that what we're really hoping for?"

Now mind you, God wants that for us also. Of all the people in the world, God wants HIS children to love life and to see good days. Somehow, we think when we come to Christ that our lives will end up in one of two camps: Either we erroneously think that all our troubles will dissipate once we are saved or we think that we are to somehow hate our existence in this life... Not so! God wants us to live a good life, but He wants us to do it in the fullest sense of that concept.

See the word "life" in verse ten? It means more than just being alive biologically. The Greek language had a word for that: "bios." It's the word we get biology from. Bios simply means living as opposed to being dead. However, bios is not the word used here in 1 Peter. The Greek word translated life" in our text is "zoe". [33] Zoe is more about the kind of life we live. It infers a life that has meaning, purpose, and a sense of fulfillment. It's a life that brings personal satisfaction.

I want to let you in on a little secret here: There's nothing wrong with desiring that! If you have somehow gotten the idea that once you become a Christian, you are supposed to be miserable and hate life, the Word of God teaches us that belief is categorically false! You are encouraged to live a life that brings fulfillment. Yet the truth is, most people never find that level of fulfillment. They never experience genuine happiness, and I believe it's because they search for it in all the wrong places.

The good life, to them, is found in chasing things, pursuing objects, and acquiring them, some of which happen to be other people used for their own self-satisfaction.

Many others find the good life in the pursuit and acquiring of money, houses, cars, clothes, vacations, sex, drugs, alcohol, food, entertainment, sports, hobbies, careers, status, education: anything that allows them to live however they wish to without guilt or responsibility. The good life is found, for them, in a pursuit of pleasure. They're always looking for something more to stoke the fires within because the acquisition of the last desire has now left them dull and wanting. So, they need to find a new thing and spend their lives in that hopeless, never-ending cycle.

We can even find people like this in the pages of Scripture.

In the Old Testament, there was one such man who was known for his avarice, his materialism. In fact, he was known for pursuing the good life with a vengeance via the same type of things, acquiring money, horses, chariots, houses, land, buildings, livestock... His name was Solomon, and he was a king of Israel and the son of King David.

He had status, power, prestige, and all the education one could imagine. He's described as immersing himself in sensual pleasure through sex, alcohol, wild parties... (He didn't so much as go to parties, as he WAS the party!) So much so that when the Queen of Sheba, from what would be modern-day Ethiopia, paid him a visit, 1 Kings 10:5 records that the sight of all of Solomon's wealth, took her breath away!

But the question we're interested in answering is "Was he content? Did he really love life when everyone went home and he was left alone with just himself for company? Did he really see what he considered good days?" Listen to his very own words for the answer. They are found in a book of the Bible he wrote called Ecclesiastes. Specifically, we'll take a look at chapter two, beginning in verse ten.

> I denied myself nothing my eyes desired; I refused my heart no pleasure. My heart took delight in all my labor, and this was the reward for all my toil. Yet when I surveyed all that my hands had done and what I had toiled to achieve, everything was meaningless, a chasing after the wind; nothing was gained under the sun.

> Then verse seventeen for the result: "So I hated life..." (NIV).

Some of you need to listen to Solomon... because he caught everything you are chasing. And when he caught it, he said it was empty, vain, and unfulfilling... But we always think it won't be the same for us. No, instead what we do is assume that the other guy didn't catch or didn't acquire enough, or he was flawed. "That's why he wasn't happy! I just want enough to be comfortable." We're masters at self- deception; and so the cycle continues on and on.

However, there is a formula for happiness and it isn't found in the words of a song, or some philosopher's musings; rather, it's found in the pages of the Word of God.

In chapter three of 1 Peter verses eight to twelve, , the apostle Peter lays out "eight" disciplines that produce a life truly worth living... a life filled with good days.

Again, the point is this: Your true happiness is a choice! It's not by chance. In other words, happiness isn't a result of what you get out of life. Happiness is a result of a mindset you bring to life! If we want to love life and see good days, we have to learn to control our minds in order to practice these specific disciplines. Five of these are found in verse eight.

1. Embrace Sound Doctrine: "Finally, all of you live in harmony with one another." Peter is appealing for believers to "all be of one mind." That phrase "live in harmony" comes from one compound Greek word, "homophron", which is comprised of two Greek words: homos meaning one and the same and "phren" meaning mind, understanding. Homophron means of the same mind, like-minded. [34]This isn't some emotional appeal for relational unity. No! This command is an appeal for unity in what we believe in; doctrinal oneness.

As children of God, we should seek to grow in the knowledge of the truth! And once we discover that truth, we are to embrace it! We are to hold on to it because it is essential to your happiness.

I know some of you are thinking, "Ok, this is where I tune this dude out." But please listen to me here. Knowing truth, understanding sound doctrine, and embracing it leads to peace, happiness, and freedom because it eliminates confusion! That thought reminds me of an old Peanuts comic strip featuring Lucy and Linus.

PEANUTS © 1965 Peanuts Worldwide LLC. Dist. By ANDREWS
MCMEEL SYNDICATION. Reprinted with permission.
All rights reserved.

Lucy: Boy, Look at it rain... What if it floods the whole world?

Linus: It will never do that...in the ninth chapter of Genesis, God promised Noah that would never happen again and the sign of the promise is the rainbow.

Lucy: You've taken a great load off my mind.

Linus: Sound theology has a way of doing that! 35

Sound doctrine, knowing the Word of God, being sure of what you believe is one of the most fundamental disciplines for true happiness! I used to tell my church in Virginia, "Live like you say you believe." Why would I say that? Because if you live like you say you believe, it will guide your days, your decisions, your relationships and conversations, etc... Listen, you'll never love life and you'll never know good days until you know and embrace doctrinal truth as taught in Scripture.

2. Show Sympathy: "Finally, all of you, be like minded; be sympathetic." Sympathetic comes from the Greek "sumpathes". It's another compound word, where the prefix "sum" means beside and "pathes" means to feel for, to suffer with. The idea is coming alongside others and feeling their feelings with them. [36] We are to have sympathy for one another, and we are to be sympathetic toward the lost also. We should be known as a people who have a burden for their lost souls! Who sympathize with their great need!

3. Love One Another: "Love" from the Greek "philadelphos", pertains to love or affection for other believers. [37] Simply put, care for one another. This requires you to be a part of a fellowship, not just to attend the fellowship. You can't just be marginally connected and truly love one another. You spend time with those whom you love, plain and simple.

4. Be Compassionate: "Finally, all of you, be like minded; be sympathetic, love as brothers, be compassionate." That word "compassionate" comes from the Greek "eusplanchnos", which literally means possessing a disposition that leads to mercy. [38] In our context, it means to feel deeply in your soul for those who are needful and for those who are unsaved. It is a more intense and visceral level of sympathy.

5. Be Humble: "Finally, all of you, be like minded; be sympathetic, love as brothers, be compassionate and humble." Humble is translated "tapeinophron" means to have a friendly, courteous mindset, to consider others as more important, to be humble-minded. [39]

So, if you want to be happy and see good days, discipline your mind to:

1. Embrace Sound Doctrine
2. Be Sympathetic
3. Actively and Regularly Participate in True Fellowship
4. Be Compassionate
5. Live with Humility

CHAPTER 14

STILL SEEKING GOOD DAYS

Some time ago, probably back twenty years or so, a friend of mine told me a story about the first time he went white- water rafting. It was either North Georgia or Tennessee, and it was supposed to be this long, scenic trip through the mountains. In fact, he said the river ran along some of the most beautiful scenery he had ever experienced but their excursion would also take them into powerful category 4-5 rapids! Very aggressive, turbulent waters, which could easily toss a person, or even worse, sink a raft!

Before they began, he said they were introduced to their guide, a young, college-aged kid who'd evidently grown up on that river and knew it well. My friend told me that before they even entered the raft, this kid was issuing instructions to everyone who would be taking the trip together in his raft with him.

He told them they, in his opinion, would see some of the most spectacular places in nature as they drifted down stream. He also warned of the impending rapids and their inherent danger. But he also said that the rapids could be enjoyable if they did two things: #1) they had to have complete confidence in their guide. And #2) they must follow his instructions. Failure on the first point would lead to failure on the second point and could turn a enjoyable day into a really bad day quickly.

My friend said for the most part, everyone did exactly that. Of course, on a few occasions, someone would ignore an instruction and they'd get tossed from the raft. But even then they were able to pull those who had been tossed out back in because they stayed the course given by the leader. The result: Everyone had a great day on the river.

I want to bring that same idea over to our desire to see good days and say this: Jesus Christ comes to each of us and says, "I want to lead you as you make this journey down the river of life." He says: "You'll pass through still quiet waters, between basins of peace and wonder-filled turns... but there are also turbulent waters ahead! Perilous rapids of trouble, but even these troubles can be joyful if you do two things: #1) You must place your complete trust in Me as your Savior. Then, #2), once you have been saved, you must follow My directions, laid down in My word at every turn."

Now, that is exactly what the apostle Peter is trying to get across to his readers in 1 Peter 3:8-12. The entire theme is summed up in the first words of verse ten: "For whoever would love life and see good days."

Incidentally, my friend told me as they made their way down river, one group of teenagers decided to completely ignore the directions of their guide. He said about two miles into the trip, they evidently passed on the wrong side of some large rocks where the water crested high off of the boulders and as they did, the water crested over the edge of the raft and it immediately sank! They went from experiencing a really good day to a miserable one in the blink of an eye. They transitioned from having a great time to pointing fingers, complaining, and just wanting the day over with!

I don't know but that sounds an awful lot like a lot of people making their way through this life. They're miserable, complaining, and discontent with life and generally just want it over with.

We looked at five things last time from verse eight. Now we're going to tackle the remaining two.

6. Don't Retaliate: In verse nine of 1 Peter 3, we're taught, "Do not repay evil with evil." This is a call to abstain from being known for having an angry disposition. Have you ever met some people who always seemed to be angry? That's what's in mind here.

The word "evil" has two implications: The first has to do with the "doing" of an act that is inherently bad or wrong. Secondly, it goes behind the act to the attitude that birthed it, to the intent and motivation behind the response.

Now, just to refresh our memories... Christians, to whom this letter was first written, were considered enemies of the Roman Empire. They were treated unjustly by the government, by their employers, by their neighbors, and even by their own families. They were hated with a vengeance. In terms of worldly possessions, they were poor because their employers paid them an unfair wage... Some were tortured; others were murdered.... Evil was a disposition of the Roman way of life. And don't you know that the urge was strong for these persecuted Christians to want to retaliate, to pay back for all the wrong done to them?

In the south people have a way of saying something derogatory towards someone without it seeming to be rude. In fact, it's almost been elevated to an art form! For example, when a person wants to put someone in their place they might say something like "Well bless their heart..." and then follow up with whatever it is the person has seemingly done wrong. Bless in this sense isn't a nice thing! So back to the recipients of this letter from the Apostle Peter; how do we know they most likely wanted to retaliate? Because today we know its human nature to want bless somebody out just for cutting us off in traffic, let alone someone who is genuinely persecuting us. Yet in the face of all of that, notice the scriptural command: "Do not repay evil with evil." That word "repay" means to pay back. For instance, it could be used for paying back a loan. In this context, it has a more sinister connotation. It's about getting even! It's referring to repaying someone in the same severe manner that you feel you were treated by them. News flash! God's Word strictly forbids that.

Recall Jesus' Sermon on the Mount from Matt. 5:38-45 (ESV)

> You have heard that it was said, "An eye for an eye, and a tooth for a tooth." But I say to you, do not resist an evil person; but whoever slaps you on your right cheek, turn the other to him also. If anyone wants to sue you and take your shirt, let him have your coat also. Whoever forces you to go one mile, go with him two. Give to him who asks of you, and do not turn away from him who wants to borrow from you. You have heard that it was said, "You shall love your neighbor and hate your enemy." But I say to you, love your enemies and pray for those who persecute you...

Trying to get even with someone consumes incredible amounts of energy, time, and mental strength. You've been there: someone treats you in a wicked manner and subsequently you find yourself lying awake at night musing over it, replaying the conversation in your mind 1,000 times. Consequently, you find yourself consumed with figuring out a way that you can even the score for the hurt they've inflicted. It never ends because the deed cannot be undone and you, seemingly, can't let it go.

Imagine with me that in each of our heads is a slot for a hard drive, like what comes in your computer. And onto this hard drive you record videos, ideas, thoughts, events, and recollections of things that have transpired.

People who are bitter are addicted to accessing that hard drive in their heads. They recount some evil or injustice done to them! They go to their thought partitions and pull out some event. "Look what she did, Look how they ridiculed me; listen to how nastily he spoke to me," and then they play that part over and over and over... Each time they replay that portion, the net effect is anger, bitterness, hate, strategizing for retaliation, and making plans to get even. If you want to hate life and see miserable days, then just make that the norm for dealing with those who mistreat you.

Want a good word? Proverbs 22:24-25 (NIV) tells us, "Do not befriend angry people or associate with hot-tempered people, or you will learn to be like them and endanger your soul." Watch out! People who are pervasively angry and bitter are contagious! Anger spreads like COVID-19. And it is easily caught!

You know exactly what I'm talking about. In your office, there's that one person who is always upset they got passed over for the promotion or recognition. They are constantly deriding the boss or the employee who did get the promotion every chance they get. Most of the time they're subtle in their derision, but pretty soon they have a little flock of followers who begin to agree with them, resulting in division and strife among the team.

In his autobiography, baseball player Billy Martin, who played baseball with the New York Yankees during their glory days, told about going hunting in Texas with Mickey Mantle. Evidently, Mickey had a friend who would let him hunt on his ranch during the off- season.

When they reached the ranch, Mickey told Billy to wait in the car while he checked with his friend. The man quickly gave his permission, but he asked a favor of Mickey in return. It seemed the man had a mule that had gone blind but he didn't have the heart to put the animal down so he asked Mickey to shoot the animal for him.

Well, the story goes that Mantle agreed to do it and was returning to the car to get his gun, but on the way, he decided to play a little trick on Billy. When he reached the car, he pretended to be angry! He scowled and slammed the door. Mantle said to Billy Martin, "My friend won't let us hunt! I am so mad at that guy! I'm going to out to his barn and shoot one of his mules!"

He drove like a maniac out to the barn. Martin protested, "Mickey, we can't do that!" But Mantle was adamant, "Just watch me," he shouted over his shoulder as he stormed into the barn, out of Martin's sight and shot the mule.

However, as he was turning to return to the car, he heard two shots outside. He ran back to the car and saw Billy in a field with his rifle in his hand. "What are you doing, Martin?" he yelled. Martin yelled back, his face red with anger,. "We'll show him! I just shot two of his cows also!" [40]

I don't know if that really happened or not but it makes a great story! Point? Anger is contagious! And once you catch the anger disease, you can say goodbye to loving life and seeing good days because your days from then on will be consumed with strife and bitterness and complaining and finger-pointing and sullenness. So, if you want to love life and see good days, then you must resist the anger that wants to retaliate, reject it, and flee from it.

7. Don't Strike Back Verbally: "Do not repay evil with evil or insult with insult." The word "insult" carries the idea of hurting or injuring someone with words.

We've all experienced that. Someone lashes out at you verbally or speaks harshly, and the tendency is to return fire with both barrels! Right? But in truth, we're instructed to respond with a blessing toward them instead. To be sure, it is hard, isn't it? I've had days when people have blessed me out for something or another I failed to do or did do that I shouldn't have. And to be perfectly honest, and to my shame, my first inclination is to get defensive and to lash out. However, God tells us that when we obey this command and adopt this attitude of humility, we will inherit a blessing.

There've been many times when people in the churches I've served have spoken harshly toward me. Sometimes it's because they are hurting over something completely outside of anything I've done, but I just get to be the lucky recipient. Other times it's because of a genuine disagreement over something. I can tell you the times that

I've been able to resist returning evil for evil and insult with insult have been wonderful times of blessing for me. After the person leaves, I generally feel a sense of peace knowing that I've represented Christ well in that situation. But even beyond that, it's amazing how God will bless me even further by soon after bringing someone into my life with an encouraging word for the ministry and me.

The point is when you allow someone to incite you to the point of retaliation, you are giving them the power to steal your joy! You're giving them the power to rob you of your love for life and to make your days miserable.

One time back when we were serving a church in Virginia, I sold my truck. I had been searching for a new to me one and finally found one in Chesapeake that I knew would be exactly what I was looking for. So, I contacted the owner and arranged to go see it. Cara and I drove ninety minutes, only to be told it had been sold out from under me. I wanted to let this guy have it! Instead, I listened to the Spirit speaking to me, and I chose to bless him and congratulate him for selling his truck.

Now to be sure, I did tell him I was frustrated that we had driven so far when he knew we were coming... but God blessed me with a wonderful remainder of the day with my wife — we took a romantic cruise together (ok, it was a ferry across the James River), ate a romantic dinner, and then shared a romantic time over dessert. God blessed me when I chose to bless someone who had done me wrong! If we had purchased that truck or I had chosen to chew the guy out, we never would've had those experiences because we would've been driving home with our new vehicle, or I would've been so mad that I would've been lousy company.

Instead bless them, pray for them, thank them, and then watch how God blesses you and helps you to see good days!

CHAPTER 15

WEARINESS OF THE SOUL

I was living in South Florida on August 24, 1992, as Hurricane Andrew roared onto the mainland. My wife and I gathered up our daughter and headed a few miles west, from the coast where we lived, to my parents' house. Packing Category 5 force winds and at least an 18' storm surge, it was the most devastating storm in US history. Estimates of upwards of 2,000 tornadoes were spawned from its ferocious winds. Andrew was so powerful that grass was literally ripped from the ground. What once were lush green landscapes were now reduced to just barren dirt. So devastating was the destruction that people who lived through it began to mark their lives by a simple acronym: "BA" (Before Andrew).

Unlike Hurricane Andrew, whose damage was predominantly caused by hurricane force winds and the tornadoes it spawned, Hurricane Katrina did most of her horrific damage as a result of water. Initially formed as a tropical depression in the waters of the Caribbean,

Katrina officially was declared Category 2 hurricane just days later. It subsequently weakened to a tropical storm as it passed over the Florida Peninsula. Then upon reaching the warm waters of the Gulf of Mexico, Katrina re-energized. By August 27, Katrina was now a strong Category 3 hurricane.

On the morning of August 29, Katrina began to batter the Gulf Coast. Biloxi, Mississippi was right in its path and sustained severe damage. However, the city of New Orleans, Louisiana experienced the worst of the storm. In the end, it wasn't the wind that caused the extensive damage to the city and surrounding area. No, instead, a levee broke in and allowed a surge of floodwater to begin pouring into the city. Like dominoes in a line, additional levees began to fail as the floodwaters overtook them. These levees were poorly designed and poorly erected. Estimates of at least 10 percent sand composition, instead of Louisiana clay, were ruled as a primary reason for the levee failures. While the storm itself was certainly catastrophic, by the time the eye passed to the southeast of the city, winds were only at Category 1 status.

The major destruction from the hurricane was due to the failures in the levees of the drainage, navigational canals, and the flood walls themselves. These elements were part of an elaborate system designed to protect the city and its residents from the effects of a major storm. However, upon later investigation, it was determined that many of the levees failed prior to their designed thresholds.[41]

Basically, two things transpired in these levees and flood walls.

1. The levees absorbed and absorbed water from the storm until the next drop of water proved to be the one drop too many, and the drainage levee began to fail catastrophically! 2. Other levees were overrun by the floodwaters released by the first levee failure and, as a result, they failed also. The end result was much of the city of New Orleans being up to 15' underwater.

Now, with that visual in mind, let me bring our discussion over to the topic at hand. When we face the unrelenting forces of weariness, we have two possible reactions: become unstable and erode into sin, or remain stable by following the example of Christ.

Let me try and put that statement into some type of context for us. When I left the church I served in Miami, I felt totally lost. To be totally honest, it still impacts me today. I had spent almost twenty-one years serving the people there, and I loved it! But when I was no longer on staff, I had no idea what to do with myself on Sundays. I felt completely useless and of no value. Now before you all go off on me regarding healthy self-esteem and job-home life balance and everything, please understand that once you are called into ministry, you cannot ever imagine yourself doing anything else. And to one day find yourself doing "anything else" is devastating. There is a sense of loss that is overpowering and debilitating.

We are all constantly under the threat of the rains of depression, conflict, frustration, and pressures at home, in our families, and on our jobs. We feel financial pressure deal with traffic jams, deadlines, discouragements, and health issues. And now to top it all off, the coronavirus too!

These forces threaten to rain on you like an endless downpour. You absorb and absorb until your soul can absorb no more. Suddenly you reach a point of total soul saturation and your soul within becomes unstable. It is at exactly this point that conditions are ripe for spiritual erosion in your life. Your soul is where the battle against good and evil is waged. It is the place where temptation is withstood. And if your soul becomes unstable the very next thing, sometimes, no matter what it is, can trigger a bad decision that can change the trajectory of your life forever.

But there is hope! Because our Lord Jesus KNEW what it was to be saturated with pain, stress, sorrow, soaked with anxiety, and drenched with weariness. Yet, His soul never became unstable! In fact, it was in incredible, heart-wrenching sorrow, His body overloaded with pain, that He accomplished the most!

It's how the people who first received this letter felt. They were saturated and weary. Remember who these recipients were? They were Jewish by race and Israel was their homeland. Seemingly no other race of people has suffered persecution like the Jews. Holocaust after holocaust has been executed upon them. They've suffered under the Egyptians, Assyrians, Babylonians, Medes,

Greeks, Romans, and Germans — All of whom sought the genocide of the Jewish race.

This letter came to them around the year AD 70 — which was an awful year to be a Jew because it was under the Romans that the Jews suffered, what is arguably, their worst persecution.

In AD 63, the Roman General Pompey captured Jerusalem. In AD 66, the first Jewish revolt was begun. The Jewish revolutionaries were able to drive the small Roman garrison from the city. In response, the Roman Emperor Nero sent General Vespasian to quell the rebellion. He was mostly successful in that he was able to force the Jewish revolutionary army back into Jerusalem itself. In AD 69, upon Nero's death Vespasian was installed as emperor. Subsequently he sent his eldest son Titus, also an accomplished general, along with thousands of troops to finish the job. According to Josephus, a Jewish historian, in the end, 1,100,000 Jews were brutally massacred. After the assault, the Romans drove the surviving Jewish peoples out of the land of Israel with the knowledge that they were strictly forbidden to ever return.

These Christian Jews who first received this little letter from the apostle Peter had just lost their nation, homes, jobs, income, security, and even loved ones in the massacre. Life is just incessantly raining discouragement and disappointment down on them. And because anti-Semitism was rife in the ancient world, Jews suffered racial persecution and wherever a Jew settled, he was hated. But as if that wasn't enough, these Christian Jews were suffering religious persecution because the Roman

Empire had made a formal commitment to persecute Christians. As a result, these early Jewish believers were robbed, raped, and tortured without cause or remorse. Consequently, they were reeling, and their souls were mentally and emotionally saturated.

Here's the danger for us: When you reach the point of total mental and emotional saturation, the net effect is weariness of your soul. And mind you, not just any ordinary weariness. No, this is a deadening fatigue of your mind, body, and soul! This phenomenon isn't unique or new. People have dealt with this since the beginning of time. Job, from the Old Testament, knew that kind of weariness, declaring in Job 10:1 (NIV), "My soul is weary." King David in Psalm 6:6 states, "I am weary with groaning."

This is exactly the place emotionally where these Christian Jews were. They were totally saturated, weary, and unstable like those rain-soaked levees of New Orleans.

Let me add it's where some of you are emotionally right now. And it's probably why you picked up this book in the first place. The rains of disappointment, failure, pressure, and people letting you down have just saturated your soul until you feel like you cannot absorb anymore.

I want you to know that Jesus Christ, the Second Person of the Trinity, the guardian of your soul, knows fully well where you are. He also fully understands the weariness you are enduring. Because He knows and understands, you can take comfort in knowing that you are not going through your circumstances alone.

In 1 Peter 3:18, we read, "For Christ died..." Jesus' physical body died when He absorbed so much sorrow, grief, hurt, loss, sadness, and weariness ... it killed Him. To be sure, He suffered great physical abuse at the hands of the Jewish leaders and the Roman army. But I believe that His heart was broken for the world, not just emotionally but physically broken as well. I believe that His level of sorrow was so great that it literally ruptured His heart!

After Jesus died, John 19:34 records that while He, Jesus, was still hanging on the cross, one of the soldiers pierced His side with a spear, releasing a sudden flow of blood and water. This is particularly telling because a corpse doesn't normally bleed. To be sure Jesus has already died before the stabbing with the spear, it's recorded that this was done to ensure that Jesus had in fact already expired! The physiological explanation of the water and blood flowing from Jesus' spear pierced side is a result of a ruptured heart. His heart muscle literally tore apart.

> The Journal of American Medical Association doctors described this phenomenon: Heart rupture occurs from physiological causes, which stem from great, emotional anxiety. The immediate cause is a sudden and violent contraction of one of the ventricles, usually the left, on the column of blood moving into it... the blood pressure reacts against the ventricle itself, which is consequently torn open... The

> blood then collects in the paracardium and soon divides itself into its two constituent parts: namely a pale, watery liquid called serum and a soft clotted substance of deep red color.[42]

That sounds exactly like what gushed out of Jesus' side when the soldier stabbed Him with a spear. The sadness and weariness of soul literally broke Jesus' heart. But He never became unstable; His determination to remain true to His Father's will never eroded.

I was out watering the lawn the other day. We had a section in the backyard that had been overrun with ground ivy and it looked terrible. The rest of the yard was beautiful, nicely manicured, green grass. (I can say that because I'm not taking any credit for it. There is a service that comes each week or so to take care of the lawn.) Anyway, removing the ivy was not a part of their regular maintenance. So, Cara and I decided to go out one weekend and remove it. The Georgia sun was hot but we persevered and eventually got all of it removed, and the soil smoothed over. The next week I bought some grass seed and peat moss and spread it over the offensive area in hopes that one day, grass will grow to match the rest of the lawn. Well, one of the things you have to absolutely do after planting grass seed is water religiously. I mean every day with no days off! This has to go on until the seed has taken root and the grass is sufficiently developed to be able to withstand the hot Georgia sun. We don't have a nozzle on the end of the hose that is dedicated to the back yard. Therefore, I stand there with my thumb over the flow of water and make my own jet stream to soak the seedlings.

If you've ever had to do this, one of the things you almost know without even having to think about it is wherever you aim, your thumb instantaneously knows how much pressure to apply. The closer the area to be watered, the less pressure on the flow. The greater distance away, the harder you need to press down over the end of the hose in order to make the water shoot out farther. It's almost like where you concentrate is where you get results.

Jesus was able to fulfill His mission because He kept focused on God's will and knew with certainty of His being reunited with His Father in heaven.

Just like that, your ability to effectively survive and thrive even, regardless of circumstances, is dependent upon your ability to focus on the right thing.

That's what we must do as well. Focus on Christ. Because when we place our hope in things we know we can and will one day lose... job, friends, career, loved ones, health, money, etcetera... we will eventually be unstable. However, when we place our hope in things we cannot lose... Jesus, heaven, salvation, eternity, the Word of God, His promises... we will remain stable and true to our calling!

CHAPTER 16

NAVIGATING LIFE'S TRIALS

Cara and I went to Tennessee on our honeymoon. Chattanooga wasn't our planned destination; however, how can anyone resist the lure of those billboards to "See Ruby Falls." So, we made plans to spend the night there and the next day we would explore Ruby Falls and Lookout Mountain. We really didn't have any expectations and soon found ourselves in a glass front elevator descending some 260' through a rock hewn shaft, making our way deep into the earth in order to experience this majesty known as Ruby Falls. That elevator ride should have triggered my "this isn't such a great idea meter" right there.

Flashes of my time stuck in the elevator as a youth came back to me. However, I did my best to suppress my anxiety at being in a confined space and soon we were in a large open cavern. From there, the guide takes you on a walking tour and recounts the tale of the discovery of Ruby Falls. All was well until we reached a particular spot where the ceiling closed in substantially. I'm not a big guy, and yet my head was close to the rock above me. All of the sudden, it was as if I could "feel" the pressure of 260' of solid rock and stone pressing down upon me. I did not want to be in that spot one second longer! Fortunately, the trail opened up and soon we were gazing upon the falls in all of their glory.

Colored lights illuminated the water, and it was spectacular to behold. It made the anxiety I experienced worthwhile. At least until the guide turned off the lights! Yeah, that's right, for some unknown reason that yahoo thought it would be cool for us to experience total and complete darkness. And by darkness, I mean absolute, pitch black night.

This is a level of darkness that feels thick and heavy, almost as if you would have to brush it away with your hand. It was an unnerving kind of moment. There was no seeing your hand in front of your face, let alone the trail to find the way out.

As long as there's some light at the end of our proverbial tunnel, there's no trial we can't manage to scratch our way though. But take away hope, block out the light, and the result is a disparaging, fearful grind.

Think about you and me as children of God. As long as we keep our eyes fixed on Jesus, there are no tight places we can't navigate our way through. But the moment our view of the light from the SON is blocked, instead of looking upward toward heaven, we look downward into our problems and trials. Instead of looking outward toward others, we become preoccupied with ourselves. Instead of confidence, we experience uncertainty and instead of knowing joy, fear becomes our constant companion.

Back to my story about Ruby Falls: Turns out the light switch trick is all part of the tour. The guide switched the lights back on after a few seconds (that only seemed like hours), and at that instant my frame of mind instantaneously changed! Dramatically, radically changed. My thoughts went from uncertainty to certainty, from fear and near paranoia to confidence in my coming out alive.

What made the difference in my brain? LIGHT! Now mind you, we were still inside the cave, hundreds of feet below the surface. But I can tell you with complete certainty that I experienced great joy because I could see light ahead on the trail and all that that meant — that there was a way out and an end to the darkness.

Life can sometimes be like a cave of darkness. Fear, confusion, and uncertainty leave us groping for light! As a pastor, I've done enough talking with folks along the way to know that some of you are there right now! You are in a dark trial. And the fear, panic, paranoia, and darkness are so thick you have to brush it away just to get out of bed and started each day.

If that describes you, let the words of Psalm 119:105 wash over you: "Your word is a lamp to guide my feet and a light for my path." Scripture points us to light in the midst of our life's darkness. When the deep caverns of life overshadow your joy and when the darkness of the world incites you to fear, remember there is a light that if you will fix your eyes upon it, it will turn your fear into rejoicing.

First Peter 4:12. NIV says: "Dear friends, do not be surprised at the fiery ordeal that has come on you to test you, as though something strange were happening to you."

That verse is presented to us in the form of a prohibition. "Do not" comes from a word meaning "continuously not, endlessly not." In other words: Don't ever be surprised at painful trials. This is written in the imperatival mode meaning it is a command. It's like Peter is saying, "I command you, do not ever, under any circumstances be surprised at painful fiery trials."

That word "surprised" is from the Greek xinidzo and it means to be stunned by some unexpected thing or happening, so shocking that you experience confusion and bewilderment. [43] The apostle Peter is saying, "Whatever comes your way, don't be stunned by it."

Trials do have a way of debilitating us, don't they? They can knock us down and cause us to despair. They're not easy to traverse — that's why they're called trials! But understand this is exactly what Peter is prohibiting! When painful trials come our way, we aren't to be shocked, stunned, or even surprised. In plain English, he's saying, "Don't be surprised when bad things happen." Which means the transverse must be true... view them as normal, common, and part and parcel of everyday life. We don't want that to be true though, do we? Even with all we know, deep down we still think there must be some type of formula in play to cause these things to happen to us. But the painful truth is painful trials in life are common. They are normal.

Somewhere along the way I've heard it said that "if you view the Christian life as some sort of walk through the roses, you're going to find yourself stuck with a lot of thorns!" You'll be painfully disappointed. Becoming a Christian, choosing to follow Jesus, and dedicating your life to Him doesn't make you immune to painful experiences.

"But rejoice..." (1 Peter 4:13 NIV) Don't be shocked and don't be stunned; instead rejoice! View your trials through the proper perspective. Understand though this is only possible by seeing things through an eternal lens. "But rejoice inasmuch as you participate in the sufferings of Christ, so that you may be overjoyed when His glory is revealed." (1 Peter 4:13 NIV)

That phrase "when His glory is revealed" moves us into the future when Jesus' glory is fully revealed to the entire world! When Jesus came to earth the first time, His glory was veiled. It was hidden in order that His purpose might be fulfilled. What purpose? Luke 19:10: "The Son of man came to seek and to save that which was lost."

At some point in the future, Scripture teaches that Jesus will return. At that time, His glory will be unveiled and uncovered. Peter is saying lift up your eyes from the trials, and dark problems of this current time, and fix your mind on the glorious, marvelous light of Jesus Christ that will one day be revealed for all the world to see. By doing this, Peter is sort of lifting our chins and, therefore our eyes also, toward heaven. He's saying look toward that glorious light to be revealed! When the world presses in, meditate on that truth.

Your world may be a dark cavern now and the trial may be hard, but there is an end. There is light! There is an exit to these painful trials you endure. I know that some of you are in some difficult, trying trials. Don't let them stun you, shock you, confuse you... nothing you are going through is unknown to God. He loves you. Begin to look at your life in the light of eternity and all that you are heir to, and let God mature your faith in the process. One day, Jesus will "flip the switch" on this life. When that happens, all the painful memories will be swept away in His glorious light!

CHAPTER 17

ENDURING THROUGH
YOUR TRIALS

I don't know about you, but I always enjoy watching the Olympics. It doesn't matter if it's the Summer or Winter Games either. I just enjoy the games. For example, I recall the 1976 US Boxing Team. Sugar Ray Leonard, Leon and Michael Spinks, Leo Randolph & Howard Davis all won gold medals that year. Spectacular! And then the 1980 Winter Olympics when the Miracle on Ice and the US hockey team beat the, until then, undefeated Soviet Union and then went on to win the gold medal!

But honestly, one of the most compelling memories I have of any Olympics comes from 1984 because I will probably NEVER forget one lady who ran the women's marathon. Her name was Gabriela Andersen-Schiess. At the time she was thirty-nine years old and held dual citizenship in the United States and Switzerland. She was living in the US and working as a ski instructor, but she participated in the games for her home country of

Switzerland. Joan Benoit went on to win this first-ever Women's Olympic Marathon, but it was Andersen-Schiess that was most remembered from that day.

It seems that everyone was running for second place. Benoit had outpaced the pack and showed no signs of slowing. This wasn't Andersen-Schiess' first marathon either. She had run very respectable times in other races, so she was not a novice. However, she was in the middle to the latter portions of the pack. When she finally entered the tunnel to begin her last circuit around the 400-meter track, it was absolutely gut-wrenching to watch.

After the race, it was determined that she was suffering from heat exhaustion. To the viewer, it looked as if she was experiencing some sort of palsy, as one side of her body no longer seemed to respond. She staggered and drunkenly tottered her way onto and around the track. Attendants quickly came up to her, but she veered away from them before they could touch her. If they had, she would have been disqualified from the race. She had come this far, and she was determined to finish. Each step was slow, painful, and agonizing, and I was only watching! Her coach and the medical personnel couldn't touch her, that is true, but that doesn't mean that they didn't do anything. They encouraged her and cheered her on. They did so in front of millions watching on TV and tens of thousands in the stands. "Keep going! You can make it! You're almost there!" The crowd in the Olympic Stadium stood to their feet, cheering and applauding. They shouted encouragements and it seemed as if they were willing her to the finish line. Finally, after what seemed like forever, she crossed the finish line and collapsed into the arms of her coach and trainer. [44]

She didn't win any medals that day, but she did win the hearts of millions and millions of people across the globe. Why? Why would people applaud the person who didn't win, or for that matter, even place? I believe it is because we admire people who finish what they start, don't we? We love to see and hear stories of how people overcome and endure to the end. And this dear lady certainly did that!

Now... in this text that we're going to deal with in this final chapter, the apostle Peter wants to talk to us about having that same kind of commitment as Gabriela Andersen-Schiess, but to Christ! He is imploring us to have the kind of commitment that sticks to it, even when the road is hard.

> However, if you suffer as a Christian, do not be ashamed, but praise God that you bear that name. For it is time for judgment to begin with God's household; and if it begins with us, what will the outcome be for those who do not obey the gospel of God; and, if it is hard for the righteous to be saved, what will become of the ungodly and the sinner? So then, those who suffer according to God's will should commit themselves to their faithful Creator and continue to do good. (1 Peter 4:16-19)

That phrase... "If you suffer" ... is a first-class conditional and that means "to assume something is true." It would be like saying, "Since you will suffer as a Christian." In other words, trials and suffering are not just part of everyday life, but trials and suffering are TIED to the Christian life! As a Christian, you will suffer. When these struggles come, you may well be tempted to quit the faith but the apostle Peter admonishes us to never quit, to never give up.

So, the question becomes, "How do we keep following when we feel so bone-wrenchingly weary, that it seems that our legs won't even support us anymore? How do we endure and keep going in the faith when life has so beaten us down with its incessant rains of discouragement and despair that we seemingly can no longer even look up, let alone get up?"

I believe there are four things found in this little section that we can take note of to help us find hope to continue, no matter what life throws our way.

1. When you are suffering, remember your future blessing.

> "If you are insulted because of the name of Christ."(1 Peter 4:14)

That Greek word translated "insulted" is oneidizo and it means to be verbally slandered, to suffer verbal abuse. I know some of you know from first-hand experience the impact that kind of attack can deliver. You know the pain of a verbal strike against your person.

Some of you may live with a spouse or other family member that verbally attacks you because of your faith in Christ. You often find yourself the target of words laced with sarcasm, which seek to ridicule your faith. These comments pierce your heart and can cause great sadness and sorrow. Still others of you face the same kind of thing in the workplace or from your friends.

So, how does a person steer a clear path through such attacks and consequently not be driven to discouragement and despair? I've been hearing of Christian musicians who are coming out and are now declaring that they are "de-vangelicals." These people who have encouraged us with their songs and lyrics are now abandoning their faith. The pressures to conform to the culture's worldview have caused them to re-evaluate what they say they believe. They have not heeded the words of the apostle Peter. Scripture says that if you suffer insult because of your commitment to Christ, you are the object of God's blessing. "If you are insulted because of the name of Christ, you are blessed for the Spirit of glory and of God rests on you." (1 Peter 4:14)

Follow my logic here: There are specific instances in Scripture when God's Spirit is said to descend and rest on someone or something. God's glory comes down and overshadows that person or thing.

For example, when the commandments were finished and delivered to Moses at Mount Sinai, Exodus 24:16, says, "The glory of the Lord rested on Mount Sinai, and the cloud covered it for six days." The glory of God rested on Mount Sinai. Then in Exodus 40 when the tabernacle was completed, the Shekinah glory of God covered the tabernacle. In 1 Kings 8 when the Ark of the Covenant was brought into the temple, the Spirit of God, the glory of God, overshadowed the temple. In the New Testament, at the scene of the baptism of Jesus, the Spirit of God descended in the form of a dove.

This resting of God's Spirit on someone or something seems to happen as an indicator of God's pleasure. With that in mind, listen again to verse fourteen: "If you are insulted because of the name of Christ, you are blessed, for the Spirit of glory and of God rests on you." So when someone takes a verbal shot at you and you feel that pain, hurt, and shame... remember the same Shekinah glory of God, which rested on Jesus, Moses, the tabernacle, the Ark of the Covenant... that same glory overshadows you because God is pleased with your commitment and the steadfastness of your faith in Him.

2. Remember God uses suffering to solidify your faith

"For it is time for judgment to begin with the household of God." (1 Peter 4:17)

At first glance, that statement doesn't seem to fit the context. Peter's been talking about suffering for Christ, how God is pleased when we suffer for His name, how the Spirit of God overshadows us when we suffer for our faith... So how does this judgment connect with suffering for Christ? Look at that word judgment... It's from the Greek "krima". It has to do with separation, dividing, partitioning off.[45] This is over here. That is over there. If you think about it, that's exactly what a judge does, isn't it? They look at evidence; they examine data and information and then decide whether the accused is guilty or innocent. Krima has that same judicial inference. It has to do with a power that separates and distinguishes.

If we take another look at our verse with this definition of krima in mind, it would make much more sense in our context. "For it is time for (a power of separation) to begin with the family of God." (1 Peter 4:17) This verse says that God has initiated some type of force that has the power to separate things in the church, to divide one form from another form, one type from another type.

So now the question for us is what has God initiated and just what is it that gets separated? I think answering the first question is right there in front of us. We've been talking about it all through this entire book... It's the idea of suffering. In verse sixteen, the apostle Peter tells us that when we suffer, we need to remember the promise of God. In verse seventeen, he shifts to explaining that this same suffering is used by God to distinguish one part of the family of God from another; precisely those who are truly saved from those in the church who are still lost. Unfortunately, not all faith is genuine and not all faith will save your soul from hell.

So, how do we know if we have true, saving faith? Peter tells us that the force of suffering makes that distinction for us. Suffering will come into your life in one

FADE

form or another... trials, hardships, persecution, but it's how we respond to these trials, hardships, and persecution that renders a verdict on the status of our souls. Once you undergo hardship, it will illicit one of two responses: It will either cause you to cling tighter and tighter to Jesus because the hardship pushes you toward Him or the pain and discouragement will cause you to turn away from Christ and your faith.

On the one hand, if your trials and suffering push you toward Christ, it validates your faith as real and genuine. But, on the other hand, if the trial causes you to pull back from your commitment to Christ, to consider yourself a "de-vangelical." you know that your faith is not real. That it is not genuine, saving faith and you won't get eternity in heaven when you die. We know this because God's Word teaches that true, saving faith is characterized by endurance. Just take a quick look at these verses for confirmation:

John 8:31 (NIV): "If you hold to my teaching, you are really my disciples."

Colossians 1:22-23: "...present you holy in His sight, without blemish and free from accusation – if you continue in your faith."

Hebrews 3:14: "We have come to share in Christ, if indeed we hold our original conviction firmly to the very end."

Hebrews 10:38-39 (NKJV): "Now the just shall live by faith...but if any man draws back, My soul shall have no pleasure in him. But we (those truly saved) are not those who draw back."

When hardships come along and a person finds him/herself abandoning his/her faith... understand, it's not that the person was saved and lost it... NO! It's that the person never had a true, saving faith to begin with. True faith endures. Back in the seventies, we had a saying... "Keep on keeping on." Child of God... no matter the hardship or trial or even persecution, keep on keeping on and God will be pleased and your faith will be rewarded.

3. Remember God uses suffering to separate those who are truly His from those who are not.

> "For it is time for judgment to begin with the household of God; and if begins with us, what will be the outcome for those who do not obey the gospel of God? And "If the righteous is scarcely saved, what will become of the ungodly and the sinner?"
> (1 Peter 4:17-18 NIV)

We just learned that God is going to allow suffering to come to His people, and He will use that very suffering to separate the true believers from the false in His church. Now Peter asks the next salient question. Namely, if God is going to do that with the church, what should we think would be the outcome for those who do not obey the gospel of God, who do not follow Christ? That's really a rhetorical question, but He expects that you already know the answer.

God permits and uses hardships to separate true from false. But, again, if God allows believers, His children, to suffer... what will be the end for those who reject His Son and His Word? Matthew 13:41-42 gives us an answer:

> "The Son of Man will send out His angels, and they will weed out (separate out) of His kingdom everything that causes sin and all who do evil. They will throw them into the blazing furnace, where there will be weeping and gnashing of teeth."

Then in verses 49-50:

> "This is how it will be at the end of the age. The angels will come and separate the wicked from the righteous and throw them into the blazing furnace, where there will be weeping and gnashing of teeth."

Don't be fooled into thinking there is some sort of inequity to this life; that somehow we are made to suffer while unbelievers prosper. No, as God's child, you aren't getting the smaller slice of the pie! Consider their end... Consider their final destination. The point is the next time you are suffering and discouraged and are tempted to think that maybe you'd be better off if you could just walk away from your faith, from your commitment to Christ... THINK AGAIN! The end for the person who doesn't obey the gospel is nothing to envy!

4. When you are suffering, remember the provision of God for His children... and endure.

"So then, those who suffer according to God's will should commit themselves to their faithful Creator and continue to do good" (1 Peter 4:19).

Peter tells us in this final thought that when you suffer, commit yourself to God, who is faithful. That word "commit" comes from a compound Greek word... "paratithemi"; para means beside, tithemi means to lay. So paratithemi means to lay something beside, to set something aside.[46] It was used to describe laying aside money or valuables for safekeeping.

Have you ever owned or rented a safe deposit box? What do you put in a safe deposit box? Things of value, right? That's the idea of the word here; something is being placed in a depository for safekeeping. The question is, what is it we are to commit?

"So then, those who suffer according to God's will should commit themselves." (1 Peter 4:19) Commit yourself! By the way, that word "themselves" psuche in the Greek[47] is a reference to the soul, the inner most part of your being. Your soul is the true you! You are to commit all of your body and soul to whom? Your faithful Creator!

God is faithful and He will deal with you faithfully. In His time, He will reward your faithfulness.

I close with one of my favorite missionary stories. It's about Henry Morrison and his wife who served for forty years in Africa. After decades of faithful service overseas, they were returning back to the States. Their hearts' desire was to stay on the field, but their age and concern over their failing health required their return to the United States. So after packing up their belongings, they boarded a steamship bound for New York.

Also traveling on the same ocean liner was a popular, well-known government official. This was none other than Teddy Roosevelt. Upon their arrival in New York, the official and his wife were greeted with great fanfare—a brass band, reporters, and photographers, even roses for his wife! In great contrast, this aged missionary couple, in failing health and having spent all of their strength in their service for Christ, walked off the gangplank and through the crowd, unmet and seemingly unknown. As they walked, a tear trickled down Henry Morris's cheek. "What's wrong?" his wife asked. Henry replied, "My whole life I've given to serving Christ. We've spent ourselves for Jesus and nobody is here to greet us. There's no bouquet of flowers for you." His dear wife thought for a minute and then said, "Honey, we're not home yet."

Child of God, when you are struggling, take heart! Remain steadfast. And remember that you're not home yet!

That simple perspective could change the way we live our lives. Jesus, wanting to draw His disciples from earth-bound living and pointless pursuits, told them that He was leaving to return to the Father, but that His leaving held a wonderful promise for them. He was going to prepare a place for them, and for us! And, what's more, He will return personally to escort us there. What an incredible promise!

That promise kept the disciples from digging their roots too deeply into the stuff of this life. The world's pleasures lost their luster in the glory of intimacy with Jesus and the fact that He would soon return for them. They endured temptation, discouragement, and trials of every kind, knowing that they weren't home yet. They lived for the moment when Jesus would return to take them to home.

We need a little more of that kind of thinking in our daily lives, don't we? It's so easy to think that this world and all it offers is all we have. It seems that the longer we are in Christ, the easier it is to drift spiritually. Remember back to when you were first saved; how your passion burned to know Him and to be known! Unfortunately, our sinful natures are bent toward making us more and more at home here. Don't be deceived; this comes at great cost to our spiritual lives. Heed the words of the apostle Paul from Philippians 3:13-14 to forget what lies behind and to press on!

So, the next time you are tempted to give up because the seeds of discontent and discouragement are trying to take root in your heart or when you are disheartened, thinking that all you have done for Jesus is in vain, just remember F.A.D.E.

Focus * Attitude * Discipline * Endurance - because, child of God, you're not home yet!

Epilogue:

To be completely honest, I've struggled to write these chapters. I'm confident in the information presented and the interpretation of Scripture. But I have to be brutally honest — it has been difficult. You see, I wrote this out of life experience. As I began to write, I was experiencing difficulties and I wasn't sure I really wanted to tackle this particular subject. It's one thing to know the right thing to do, but it's quite another to actually have to live it out in the moment. My wife and I have been in a prolonged time of trial and testing. And by prolonged, I mean years and, in some instances, decades. We've battled health issues that are debilitating. We've suffered financial hardship that impacts us even today. We have struggled emotionally as we have pleaded with God to rescue us from our circumstances. We've known it all: family, financial, job and career struggles, betrayal by close friends and colleagues. We know what it is to have friends stop calling because no matter what they've thought and prayed for — our circumstances don't seem to change. Yet, I can attest with all of my being that when you hear God whisper, "I am enough and My grace is sufficient," it is true!

After applying the lessons from 1 Peter, the Lord has granted me such peace and contentment in the midst of my trials. To be sure, the circumstances have not yet been resolved. However, I know that God will never leave me nor forsake me and no matter the outcome, I can trust in Him. Please believe me when I say these things I have tried to share with you are true. I am a living proof!

Endnotes

1 Goodman, Ryan and Schulkin, Danielle. "Timeline of the Coronavirus Pandemic and U.S. Response." *Just Security*. April 13, 2020. https://www.justsecurity.org/69650/timeline-of-the-coronavirus-pandemic-and-u-s-response/.

2 Ibid

3 Ibid

4 Ibid

5 https://www.worldometers.info/coronavirus/country/us

6 Muller, Richard and Quay, Steven. "Science Closes In on Covid's Origins." *Wall Street Journal* October 5, 2021. https://www.wsj.com/articles/covid-19-coronavirus-lab-leak-virology-origins-pandemic-11633462827.

7 MacArthur, John F., Jr. *John 1–11*. MacArthur New Testament Commentary. Chicago: Moody Press, 2006.

[8] Cherry, Kendra. "How the Fight or Flight Response Works." *Combat Stress Magazine: American Institute of Stress* August 18, 2019. https://www.stress.org/ how-the-fight-or-flight-response-works

[9] "Fight, Flight, Freeze or Fold." *BrainHarmony.com.* May 21, 2021. https://www.brainharmony.com/blog/2021/5/21/ fight-flight-freeze-or-fold

[10] Wiersbe, Warren W. *The Bible Exposition Commentary.* Wheaton, IL: Victor Books, 1996.

[11] Oates, Harry. "The Great Jewish Revolt of 66 CE." *World History Encyclopedia.* Last modified August 28, 2015. https://www.worldhistory.org/article/823/ the-great-jewish-revolt-of-66-ce/.

[12] Cross, F. L., and Elizabeth A. Livingstone, eds. *The Oxford Dictionary of the Christian Church.* Oxford; New York: Oxford University Press, 2005.

[13] Cross, F. L., and Elizabeth A. Livingstone, eds. *The Oxford Dictionary of the Christian Church.* Oxford; New York: Oxford University Press, 2005.

[14] "Nero's Persecutions Begin, A.D.64," Landmark Events, accessed December 1, 2019, https://landmarkevents.org/ neros-persecutions-begin-a-d-64/.

[15] J.M.K.C. Donev et al. (2021). Energy Education - Law of conservation of energy [Online]. Available: https://energyeducation.ca/encyclopedia/Law_of_conservation_of_energy. [Accessed: December 26, 2021].

[16] Vine, W. E., Merrill F. Unger, and William White Jr. *Vine's Complete Expository Dictionary of Old and New Testament Words.* Nashville, TN: T. Nelson, 1996.

[17] Vine, W. E., Merrill F. Unger, and William White Jr. *Vine's Complete Expository Dictionary of Old and New Testament Words.* Nashville, TN: T. Nelson, 1996.

[18] Vine, W. E., Merrill F. Unger, and William White Jr. *Vine's Complete Expository Dictionary of Old and New Testament Words.* Nashville, TN: T. Nelson, 1996.

[19] Tom Leonard, "9/11 victims who fell from Twin Towers 'appeared to be blinded by smoke," DailyMail.com, September 11, 2011, https://www.dailymail.co.uk/news/article-2035806/9-11-victims-fell-Twin-Towers-appeared-blinded-smoke.html.

[20] Naudet, Jules, Naudet, Gedeon, Hanlon, James, *9/11,* 2002, CBS Worldwide Inc.

[21] *Quotes.net.* STANDS4 LLC, 2021. Web. 26 May 2021. <https://www.quotes.net/quote/11359>.

[22] Vine, W. E., Merrill F. Unger, and William White Jr. *Vine's Complete Expository Dictionary of Old and New Testament Words*. Nashville, TN: T. Nelson, 1996.

[23] Vine, W. E., Merrill F. Unger, and William White Jr. *Vine's Complete Expository Dictionary of Old and New Testament Words*. Nashville, TN: T. Nelson, 1996.

[24] Vine, W. E., Merrill F. Unger, and William White Jr. *Vine's Complete Expository Dictionary of Old and New Testament Words*. Nashville, TN: T. Nelson, 1996.

[25] Vine, W. E., Merrill F. Unger, and William White Jr. *Vine's Complete Expository Dictionary of Old and New Testament Words*. Nashville, TN: T. Nelson, 1996.

[26] Vine, W. E., Merrill F. Unger, and William White Jr. *Vine's Complete Expository Dictionary of Old and New Testament Words*. Nashville, TN: T. Nelson, 1996.

[27] Vine, W. E., Merrill F. Unger, and William White Jr. *Vine's Complete Expository Dictionary of Old and New Testament Words*. Nashville, TN: T. Nelson, 1996.

[28] "Ancient Roman Military Clothing," Wikipedia.org, accessed November 20, 2021, https://en.wikipedia.org/wiki/Ancient_Roman_military_clothing.

[29] Vine, W. E., Merrill F. Unger, and William White Jr. *Vine's Complete Expository Dictionary of Old and New Testament Words*. Nashville, TN: T. Nelson, 1996.

[30] Vine, W. E., Merrill F. Unger, and William White Jr. *Vine's Complete Expository Dictionary of Old and New Testament Words*. Nashville, TN: T. Nelson, 1996.

[31] Lowery, Robert, "Nothing But the Blood", Public Domain, 1876.

[32] Robert Jr. McFerrin, "Don't Worry Be Happy", "Simple Pleasures", © Universal Music Publishing Group, BMG Rights Management, Songtrust Ave 1988.

[33] Vine, W. E., Merrill F. Unger, and William White Jr. *Vine's Complete Expository Dictionary of Old and New Testament Words*. Nashville, TN: T. Nelson, 1996.

[34] Vine, W. E., Merrill F. Unger, and William White Jr. *Vine's Complete Expository Dictionary of Old and New Testament Words*. Nashville, TN: T. Nelson, 1996.

[35] PEANUTS © 1965 Peanuts Worldwide LLC. Dist. By ANDREWS MCMEEL SYNDICATION. Reprinted with permission. All rights reserved.

[36] Vine, W. E., Merrill F. Unger, and William White Jr. *Vine's Complete Expository Dictionary of Old and New Testament Words*. Nashville, TN: T. Nelson, 1996.

[37] Vine, W. E., Merrill F. Unger, and William White Jr. *Vine's Complete Expository Dictionary of Old and New Testament Words.* Nashville, TN: T. Nelson, 1996.

[38] Vine, W. E., Merrill F. Unger, and William White Jr. *Vine's Complete Expository Dictionary of Old and New Testament Words.* Nashville, TN: T. Nelson, 1996.

[39] Vine, W. E., Merrill F. Unger, and William White Jr. *Vine's Complete Expository Dictionary of Old and New Testament Words.* Nashville, TN: T. Nelson, 1996.

[40] Andrew Rotondi, "Billy Martin, Mickey Mantel and the Cow Story", bronxpinstripes.com, 2019, http://bronxpinstripes.com/yankees-history/billy-martin-mickey-mantle-and-the-cow-story/.

[41] Gibbens, Sarah. "Hurricane Katrina, Explained." *National Geographic.* January 16, 2019. https://www.nationalgeographic.com/environment/article/hurricane-katrina

[42] Edwards, William D., Wesley J. Gabel, and Floyd E. Hosmer. "On the Physical Death of Jesus Christ." JAMA 255.11 (1986): 1455-1463.

[43] Vine, W. E., Merrill F. Unger, and William White Jr. *Vine's Complete Expository Dictionary of Old and New Testament Words.* Nashville, TN: T. Nelson, 1996.

⁴⁴ Unger Motivation, "Gabriela Andersen-Schiess 1984
Olympics - Nothing Left", February 27, 2016, https://www.
youtube.com/watch?v=8kdaRQtrPjo.

⁴⁵ Vine, W. E., Merrill F. Unger, and William White Jr.
*Vine's Complete Expository Dictionary of Old and New
Testament Words.* Nashville, TN: T. Nelson, 1996.

⁴⁶ Vine, W. E., Merrill F. Unger, and William White Jr.
*Vine's Complete Expository Dictionary of Old and New
Testament Words.* Nashville, TN: T. Nelson, 1996.

⁴⁷ Vine, W. E., Merrill F. Unger, and William White Jr.
*Vine's Complete Expository Dictionary of Old and New
Testament Words.* Nashville, TN: T. Nelson, 1996.